Antique & Collectible
FISHING REELS
Identification, Evaluation, and Maintenance

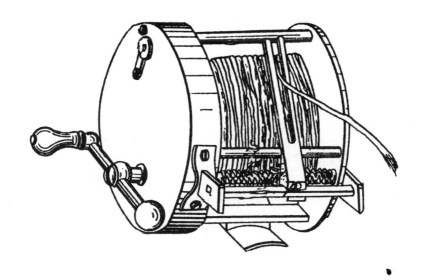

By Harold Jellison and D.B. Homel

FORREST PARK PUBLISHERS
Bellingham, Washington

FORREST PARK PUBLISHERS
P.O. Box 29775
Bellingham, Washington 98228
(360) 647-2505

PRINTED IN THE UNITED STATES OF AMERICA

ISBN 1-879522-06-3

TABLE OF CONTENTS

ACKNOWLEDGMENTS

Electronic Pre-Press ~ Cindy Matson **PMT** ~ Quicksilver Photo Lab
Illustrations ~ Harold Jellison **Foreword** ~ Hugh Lewis
Color Plates ~ D.B. Homel **B&W Photographs** ~ D.B. Homel

The authors wish to thank their families for being patient the long eighteen month necessary for compilation and completion of the text, photos, and captions. We know that it seemed as if the endless stream of reels and parts would never be put away. Additional thanks are due members of the NFLCC, with whom we have exchanged knowledge, friendship and tackle over our many years of association with that fine organization.

Frontis Page ~ *Original drawing from the patent of M.S. Palmer, February 28, 1860, depicting the first reciprocating line guide (level-wind) attached to a fishing reel.*

AUTHOR'S PREFACE

There are many and varied reasons for becoming involved with these simple to complex, "pieces of time", called fishing reels. Some individuals appear to be motivated by dollars and cents, while there are those true collectors who wonder of the companionship a reel must have brought to the person or persons who used and cared for it.

A fishing reel, "mint condition" in the original box with papers and accessories commands the highest price. However, my way of thinking is that the mint reel's place in time is limited, primarily, to the era of those who conceived the idea as to the reel's construction and carried it through to a final product. Personally, I find an old, well-used-but-not-abused fishing reel more attractive. It has served the purpose for which it was built. Consequently, its place in time has more meaning. If only it could answer the many questions that come to mind!

Occasionally we have the privilege to come across a fishing reel that emanates a beauty from within that is difficult to describe. An early Meek multiplier seems to have this quality — which can be found in certain paintings of the great masters.

Some tool collectors have the feeling that they are only the temporary custodian or keeper of the tools — which are to be shown, admired and sometimes carefully used for the purpose they were intended. This idea could well apply to fishing reel collectors.

Being totally computer ignorant, I still use index cards, pen or pencil as a means of organizing my accumulation of fishing reels. They are in alphabetical order by type (i.e. single action fly reel), by company (i.e. Pflueger), and by name (i.e. Medalist).

The cards contain the following information:

Name and model of reel
Date obtained (whether purchase or trade)
Name of seller
Cost and estimate of current market value
Any cleaning, repairs or parts made
Any obvious or hidden flaws

Last but not least, any historical background covering the questions of who, when and where. When a reel is sold or traded, the information on the card goes with the fishing reel, but the card I keep. This way the buyer is given all information relative to that reel, including honest disclosure of repairs or known defects. My card will now have the selling or trading price listed with the name of the purchaser and date. It is then filed in an index drawer, titled Sold or Traded, using the same system as above.

Dan and I do hope this book will not only increase your knowledge of collectible and antique fishing reels, but will assist you in your search to acquire fine additions to your collection at a fair and reasonable price. We wish you the best of luck in your endeavors.

One final helpful hint:

As an accumulator or collector, you can sometimes keep peace in the family by using the excuse that every new collectible reel you bring home is helping to build an annuity for your heirs!

Harold G. Jellison

FOREWORD
by Hugh Lewis

This collaboration by Harold Jellison and Dan Homel represents a real treat in the literature of sporting collectibles. These diversely talented friends share essential common interests: A love for the outdoors; a passion for fishing not merely as a sport, but also as a means of restoring balance to lives otherwise meshed of necessity into the workaday world; and an appreciation for the craftsmanship and artistry found in the construction of fishing tackle.

Harold Jellison, known affectionately as "Mr. J" to a whole generation of art students at Lynden High School in Lynden, Washington, was born at a very early age in southwest Washington, at a time when the "harvest trout", as the local sea-run cutthroat were sometimes known, still returned in substantial numbers to the Coweeman River. Young Harold could frequently be found waiting for them there, ready to roll-cast a hand-tied fly in their direction, while his adolescent contemporaries toiled away in classrooms. It was a matter of some surprise to his teachers, that some years later this intuitive truant would take a developing interest in art back to the classroom as a faculty member. Life as a teacher provided Harold with enough free time to develop an almost startling collection of antique fishing reels, many of which are portrayed in this fine book. The careful drawings, along with his thoughtful text on reel maintenance and repair, represents a true synthesis of Harold's many talents and interests.

Dan Homel was trained as a lawyer, but fortunately found a gentler path to existence, with several popular books on fishing and related topics now under his belt. With an interest in old fishing reels and photography, this collaboration with our friend Harold soon became inevitable. Dan's folksy but succinct writing style helps draw the reader willingly into what could otherwise be a morass of arcane detail. Whether the reader is already an avid collector looking to obtain an informal appraisal of a reel collection, or is just getting interested in the hobby, *Antique & Collectible Fishing Reels* should provide loads of reading satisfaction.

Hugh Lewis

BAITCASTING (MULTIPLYING) REELS

A slew of Pflueger reels and parts, appropriately topped by the famous Supreme — perhaps the most popular baitcasting reel in the history of sport fishing. A new Supreme was not cheap. Retail price was $25 as early as 1938. (Older Pflueger Akron and Pflueger Rocket at bottom).

Pflueger Trump #1943, a simple yet efficient level wind, multiplying baitcaster with jeweled bearings. This one is in the original box and was made in the 1950s. List price at that time was $3.25, a terrific buy.

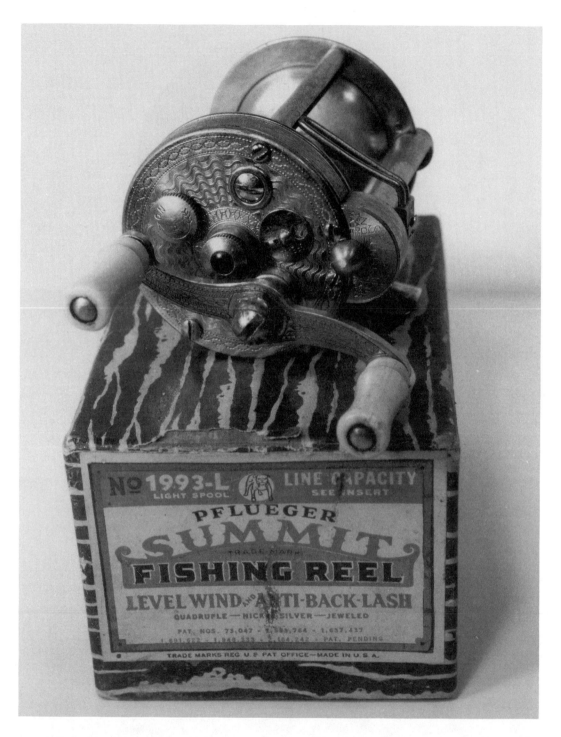

A Pflueger Summit #1993-L in the original box, made September 1946.
An easy way to date a Pflueger reel. like this, is to look at the bottom of the
box for the manufacturing date stamped in ink. The Summit, with its
engraved, almost tattoo like appearance, was a Pflueger favorite.

Rear view of a Meisselbach Cattucci #257 "Symploreel" (the words *Level Winder Non Backlash* are engraved on its face). This model is the 100 yard size. Made in Newark, New Jersey — and stamped with an August 26, 1924 patent date on the back plate. The Symploreel is equipped with a convenient push-button "takapart" feature for service and lubrication.

Meisselbach "Okey" model #625 with a quick take-apart feature, made in Elyria, Ohio. Upon casting, the unusual level-wind line guide falls forward allowing the line to flow off the spool smoothly. When retrieved, the handle is turned clockwise and the line guide retracts. It exhibits a long handle for speed. This Okey is in excellent condition.

At top is a Meisselbach #580 casting reel with a quick "takapart", flanged threaded front plate (handle side). A fairly common, but high quality non-level-wind reel circa 1910. At bottom is an Abbey & Imbrie reel that was made by Meisselbach and is identical to the reel above. Meisselbach made reels and/or parts for Abbey & Imbrie, Kingfisher, Heddon, Union Hardware and others.

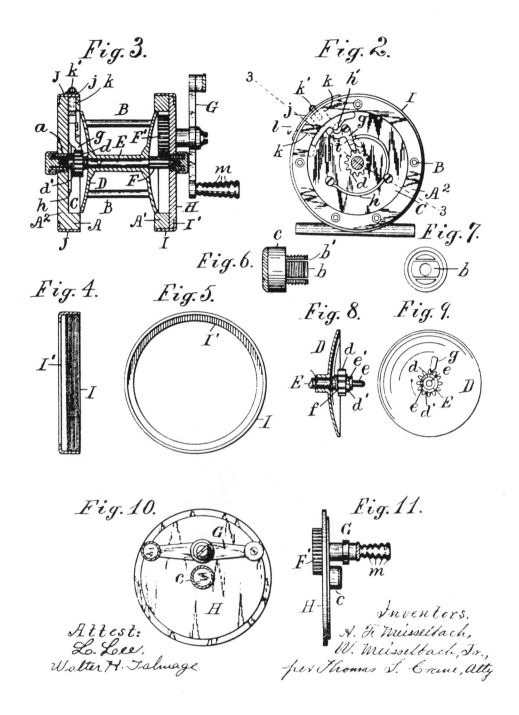

A copy of an early Meisselbach patent describing the initial invention of the famous "takapart" feature whereby the spool can be removed from the frame without the use of any tools. This facilitates examination, adjustment, and oiling of the drive and click gearing. Another feature outlined in this patent is an improved form of click (figure 2) which is actuated only when the line is running out.

A simple nickel-plated multiplying reel marked only with the name *Special*. It is in much better condition than most "no-name" reels of this type. The reel was purchase years ago from the collection of a reel maker in California It sits pictured here next to a nice South Bend diving plug.

Ocean City #970 levelwind baitcasting reel — nearly mint condition in the original shop-worn box. This is not a particularly valuable reel, but is appealing as a collectible due to its gleaming, never-been-used appearance.

Meek No.3 *Freespool* from the Horton Manufacturing Co. of Bristol, Connecticut. This distinctive reel (serial #6703) was found in excellent condition with an original leather case. The free-spool mechanism is automatically engaged when a cast is executed. A wood spool insert indicates that it may have been used for tournament casting.

No.34 Bluegrass "Simplex" Freespool multiplier made in Bristol, Connecticut by the Horton Mfg. Co. Horton bought out B.F. Meek and Sons of Louisville, Kentucky in the early 1900s. Horton products are of high quality and still considered to be "Kentucky" reels. This model 34 is almost identical to a Meek 33, with the exception of the free-spool feature.

The B.F. Meek and Sons No. 33 Bluegrass reel, made in Louisville, Kentucky. B.F. Meek had a long career as a reel maker, having been partners with his brother, Jonathan, in Frankfort, KY from 1840-1851. After another partnership with B.C. Milam, he moved to Louisville and formed a company with his sons (1883).

No. 764,348.   PATENTED JULY 5, 1904.

W. CARTER.
FISHING REEL.
APPLICATION FILED JAN. 21, 1904.

NO MODEL.

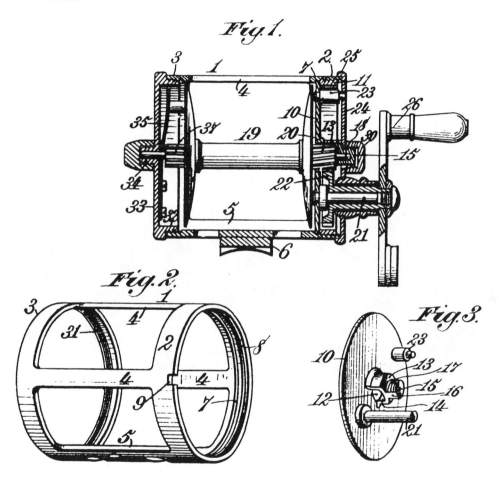

Fig. 1.

Fig. 2.

Fig. 3.

The famous Carter Fishing Reel patent of July 5, 1904 — apparent on the Meek 33. The patent application states that *The invention . . . aims to provide a fishing reel which is so constructed as to permit, when occasion requires, the removal of the spool, as well as other parts which go to make up the reel, and to also permit the ready assembly of the parts when separated.*

B.C. Milam and Son German silver multiplying reel — handmade in Frankfort, Kentucky during the 1885-1890 period. This is a No. 4 size, and has a beautiful, elongated foot and ivory winding knob. The reel is in excellent condition. Notice that the screw-heads are in nice shape and foot is unaltered, full length at both ends.

B.C. Milam and Son *Rustic No.3* high grade casting reel made in Frankfort, Kentucky between 1910 and 1920. The winding knob is celluloid. The precise, fine click mechanism is operated by a single, sliding button on the reel face. A later Milam in excellent condition.

Two Shakespeare "Leader" reels — non level wind design. The top reel has no model number, the lower reel is engraved with #3036. The model #3036 includes a red agate bearing cap, indicative of higher quality. Made in Kalamazoo, Michigan.

Early William Shakespeare Jr. *Standard* casting reel. Model is a No.2, 80 yard size, quadruple multiplier. Knurled, twin controls (friction drag and click) protruding through black, hard rubber inserts, are sandwiched between inner and outer plates. A non level-wind reel with a single counter-balanced winding knob and handle assembly. Should be graded in good to very good condition due to overall wear and some dings.

The Shakespeare *Universal* #23038 (1922 model). This non level-wind multiplying baitcasting reel sports an unusual handle shape and bulbous, counter-balance. It is in good to very good condition.

The Shakespeare *Ideal* level wind casting reel #1963. Features a knurled click control mounted between the inner and outer right plate in a black bakelite insert. It is in excellent condition and displays beautiful jeweled bearing caps. The twin winding knobs are celluloid. The original stitched, leather case has *Shakespeare* embossed on the front.

(No Model.)

W. SHAKESPEARE, Jr.
FISH LINE REEL.

No. 591,086.

Patented Oct. 5, 1897.

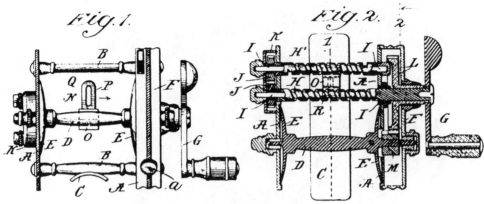

No. 853,311.

PATENTED MAY 14, 1907.

W. E. MARHOFF.
FISHING REEL.
APPLICATION FILED OCT. 22, 1906.

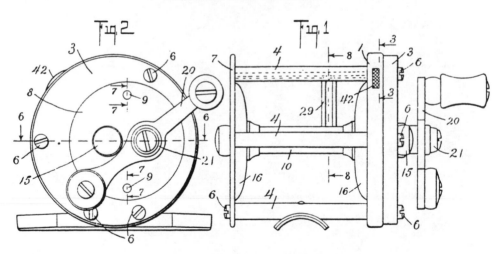

Shakespeare's level wind patents were a major asset, beginning with the 1897 double shaft mechanism (which was utilized on the rare "Style B & C" models about 1900). The 1907 W.E. Marhoff patent, purchased by Shakespeare, was the basis for many level-winds to follow. The earlier patent states . . . *means are provided for winding the line in regular even layers, similar to those found on a spool of thread.*

Shakespeare *Standard Sportcast* model #1977 GD made in 1947. A narrow spool direct drive multiplier. This specimen is in excellent condition. It is interesting to note that Shakespeare is reputed to have produced and marketed over 1000 different variations of casting reels.

SHAKESPEARE REEL PARTS DIAGRAMS with PARTS REFERENCE NUMBERS

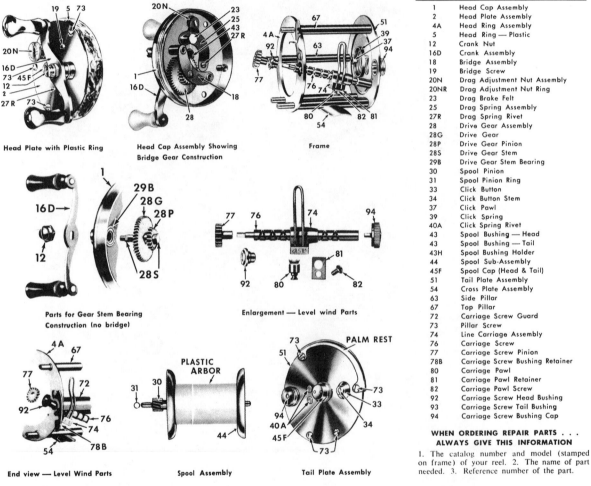

REF. NOS.	PART NAMES
1	Head Cap Assembly
2	Head Plate Assembly
4A	Head Ring Assembly
5	Head Ring — Plastic
12	Crank Nut
16D	Crank Assembly
18	Bridge Assembly
19	Bridge Screw
20N	Drag Adjustment Nut Assembly
20NR	Drag Adjustment Nut Ring
23	Drag Brake Felt
25	Drag Spring Assembly
27R	Drag Spring Rivet
28	Drive Gear Assembly
28G	Drive Gear
28P	Drive Gear Pinion
28S	Drive Gear Stem
29B	Drive Gear Stem Bearing
30	Spool Pinion
31	Spool Pinion Ring
33	Click Button
34	Click Button Stem
37	Click Pawl
39	Click Spring
40A	Click Spring Rivet
43	Spool Bushing — Head
43	Spool Bushing — Tail
43H	Spool Bushing Holder
44	Spool Sub-Assembly
45F	Spool Cap (Head & Tail)
51	Tail Plate Assembly
54	Cross Plate Assembly
63	Side Pillar
67	Top Pillar
72	Carriage Screw Guard
73	Pillar Screw
74	Line Carriage Assembly
76	Carriage Screw
77	Carriage Screw Pinion
78B	Carriage Screw Bushing Retainer
80	Carriage Pawl
81	Carriage Pawl Retainer
82	Carriage Pawl Screw
92	Carriage Screw Head Bushing
93	Carriage Screw Tail Bushing
94	Carriage Screw Bushing Cap

**WHEN ORDERING REPAIR PARTS . . .
ALWAYS GIVE THIS INFORMATION**

1. The catalog number and model (stamped on frame) of your reel. 2. The name of part needed. 3. Reference number of the part.

Captions within diagram: Head Plate with Plastic Ring; Head Cap Assembly Showing Bridge Gear Construction; Frame; Parts for Gear Stem Bearing Construction (no bridge); Enlargement — Level wind Parts; End view — Level Wind Parts; Spool Assembly; Tail Plate Assembly; PLASTIC ARBOR; PALM REST

Excerpt from a Shakespeare parts manual provides a good general description of the typical level-wind multiplier. Notice that the "end plates" are called *head plate* (front or face) and *tail plate* (back). Nomenclature for these and other parts varied from maker to maker.

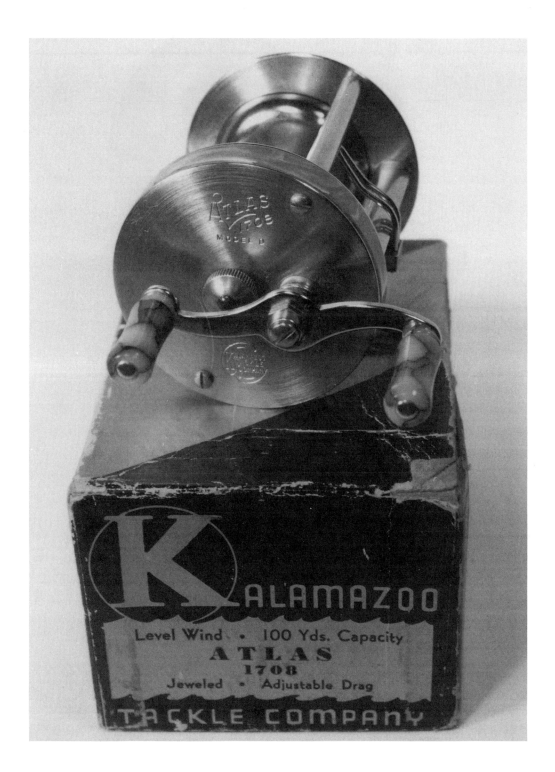

Kalamazoo *Atlas* jeweled multiplier with level-wind. A model #1708, gleaming new in the original, shop-worn box.

From Brooklyn, New York (circa 1898) — a Julius Vom Hofe casting reel of
bakelite with nickel front plate and pillars. The familiar Vom Hofe 1885 and
1889 patents are engraved on the face. An early upgrade of this model
included silver rims for durability. Notice the ornate "rosette" screw wash-
ers, and flexible "star" washer on reverse for drag adjustment.

Bronson *Modern* level-wind casting reel model #100 (c.1930), new in the original maroon box. Since it is not constructed of high grade materials, this reel might be considered cheap. However, it is impeccable in appearance, sturdily built, and smooth of operation. Would go at a premium above the "excellent" price.

A German silver, J.A. Coxe model 25-3 level-wind, freshwater casting reel produced in Bronson, Michigan. The use of bakelite as a material for the end plates was a practice adopted from the original California ocean reels produced by Joe Coxe in the 1930s. The 25-3 manifests a fine set of ivory winding knobs which are spring loaded for smooth operation.

Union Hardware *Sunnybrook* and its twin (unmarked). These sturdy, inexpensive multipliers were nickel-plated. Both reels have the standard Sunnybrook white painted winding knob, that is most always chipped.

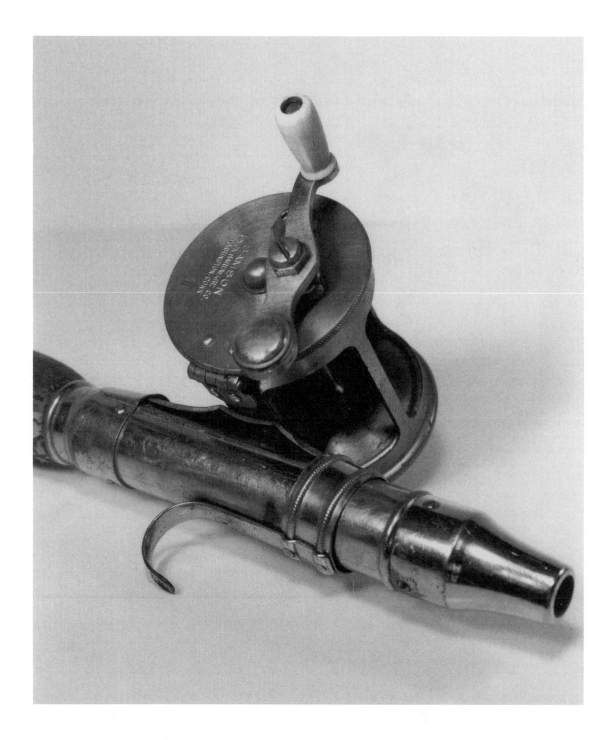

Union Hardware of Torrington, Connecticut sold this *Samson* reel which exhibits an unusual hinged take-a-part feature. The reel is attached to a Union Hardware rod of the same era (1920).

An early Union Hardware Company bakelite, level-wind casting reel. The winding knobs are an attractive carmel color and the jeweled end bearing caps are a striking shade of emerald. An apparently inexpensive reel that revolves smooth as silk. Quite alluring.

The ABU *Ambassadeur* #1750 manufactured in Sweden around 1965. A push button free-spool is located at mid-handle. Constructed of red anodized aluminum and nickel-plated brass.

A 5000 series *Ambassadeur* complete with star drag and free-spool. A top selling, modern classic. Most came enclosed in an oval shaped, leather case with extra parts, wrench, and oil. Older Ambassadeurs are popular collectibles in Europe, The U.S., Japan, and Canada.

The *Arnold Palmer* Baitcaster. An inexpensive level-wind reel produced in Japan during the 1960s by Keystone. A fun type of fishing collectible, but potentially worth more to a golf aficionado due to Palmer's likeness on the colorful box.

A mint condition level wind *Outdoorsman Castomatic* in the original box. Made by Quaker City Gear Works, Philadelphia. Constructed of hard plastic and plated brass with a steel spool shaft. An obscure maker yes, but not worth a heck of a lot.

Pair of old "children's reels" made from low quality materials. More functional as a toy than a practical fishing tool. Still, they make curious collectibles or display pieces.

FLY REELS

A tiny, but stout, solid brass single action trout reel attributable to Thomas H. Chubb. The winding knob affixed to the half-handle is hard rubber. This reel is in excellent condition and was built around 1905.

A small "jobber" reel, possibly from the Enterprise Mfg. Co. or Andrew B. Hendryx. Many of these simple, single action reels were produced from 1890 to 1910. They were packed by the dozen or half-dozen and distributed to small hardware and general stores throughout the country. Wholesale price was under $1.50 per <u>dozen</u> for a reel such as this with no click (about 12-15¢ each!).

A gleaming black bakelite, click reel of the design distributed by Montague in the 1930s. The hardware is nickel plated and rims are of a notched design. This little reel is in excellent condition.

Raised pillar trout reel similar to the Leonard style, but of lower quality. This nickel plated fly reel was made around 1910 and has a wood winding knob and counter balance handle set into the face,

An almost miniature fly reel made about 1919 when Winchester took over
Barney & Berry. Exact duplicates exist bearing *Winchester* markings, pro-
viding evidence of the transition period.

Small bronzed-brass, half handle trout reel of British origin circa 1890. The winding knob is solid brass and blackened. The reel foot is a cast design that is hand finished. Most reel feet of this nature turn up filed but the one pictured is full length.

Lucas and Walsh salmon reel of solid brass and bearing a cow horn winding knob. An ancient, heavy piece of fly fishing history from a relatively
unknown maker circa 1865-1875. The reel would be rated poor to fair for
evaluation purposed due to cosmetic wear and presence of a replacement
knob screw.

G.W. Gayle and Son Company *Simplicity No. 6* aluminum trout reel made in Frankfort, Kentucky. These mass produced single action reels are fairly common — however the early, handmade Gayle baitcasters are a rare find.

A *Bristol No. 65* fly reel made by the Horton Manufacturing Co. of Bristol, Connecticut. It is an inexpensive but reliable trout model made of aluminum with a steel lineguide. This one is in excellent condition.

Heddon #320 *Daisy* single action fly reel assembled in USA (parts made in Japan). A good, serviceable reel, similar in appearance to the *Hardy Princess* of the late 1950s. Notice the two empty holes at top of the frame; it is missing the lineguide.

Hardy of England *Sunbeam* fly reel in the original box circa 1915. Equipped with the early "horseshoe" style spool latch, a smooth brass foot, and heavy brass wire lineguide. Older Sunbeams, boxed and in excellent condition are getting harder to find.

Hardy *Perfect* ball-bearing fly reel with gray enamel finish circa 1960. Features a ribbed, brass foot and agate lineguide. This 3 5/8 inch model, with the famous adjustable *Mark II* check, was found in mint condition enclosed in a zippered, leather case. The Perfect was first cataloged in 1892. Its faceplate unscrews to facilitate spool removal.

A Hardy *St. George* 3 3/4 inch fly reel with patented agate line guide. This is an earlier model with 3 screws attaching the latch cover to the spool.

With the spool removed, the patented Hardy *Duplicated MK II* check is revealed in fine working order. Also notice the ridged or so called "ribbed" brass foot made to accommodate the wide threads on Hardy's fly rod reel seats.

Hardy's *Flyweight* machined aluminum trout fly reel with scarce "silent check". This is an earlier model in the *Lightweight* series featuring the patented 2 screw lineguide (1955-1968).

A Hardy Brothers *Uniqua* fly reel in the small 2 7/8 inch size. This Hardy (circa 1935) is equipped with the "telephone" style spool-release latch, affixed to the spool with two silver screws. A "ribbed" brass foot (which first appeared on Hardy fly reels in 1928) is evident. The reel check is non-adjustable. Despite some finish wear, a grading of excellent might be justified due to the outstanding, tight mechanical condition.

A Thompson aluminum fly reel approximately 3 3/8 inches in diameter. The check is a sophisticated ball bearing design. The exterior closely resembles the 1930-1940 era *Hardy Perfect* (also shown). The Thompson was made by Lovens Mfg. in California about 1955, and is now quite rare. Value is about twice that of the 3 3/8 Perfect.

Pflueger's economy fly reels from circa 1950-1970. The *Sal-Trout* #1554 and *Progress* #1774. Both are of simple aluminum construction with a non-adjustable click drag.

Early Pflueger *Progress* click trout fly reel. The inexpensive raised pillar, skeleton design was popular in the 1920s. This reel exhibits the familiar *bull-dog* trade mark on its foot and is in only poor-fair condition due to several maladies (not the least of which are a chewed-up knob and corrosion of the spool and frame).

An early Pflueger *Medalist* #1494 fly reel with dark blued finish and metal engraved spool release-latch cover. Notice the turned pillars and cast aluminum foot (broken) not found on later versions. This one is also missing the round lineguide commonly seen on Medalists of this age — condition is therefore rated poor.

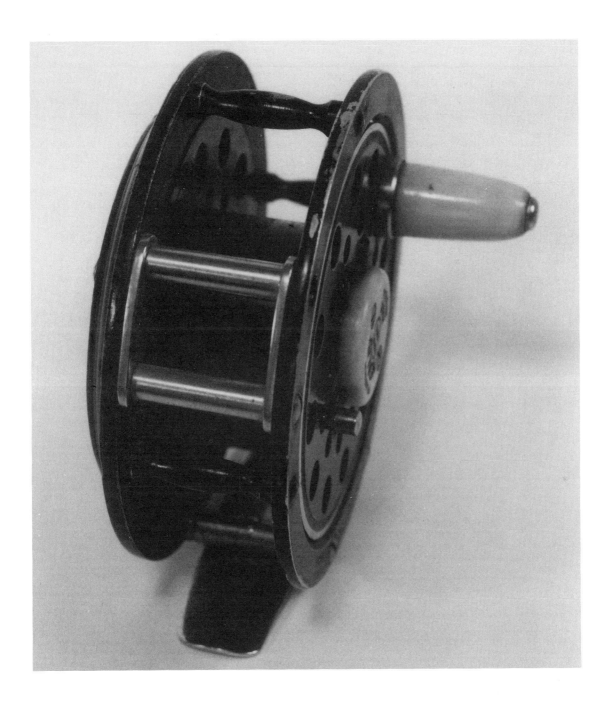

A transitional model Pflueger *Medalist* #1494 fly reel having the old style, turned pillars combined with a modern plastic spool release-latch cover and square lineguide. Look closely to make sure a newer replacement spool is not paired-up with an older frame!

Model No. 2094 Pflueger "Gem" fly reel — black enamel finish over cast aluminum. This is the first model Gem, as indicated by a crescent spool release-latch similar to the early *Hardy* mechanism.

Shakespeare *Russel* No. 1985 Model FK, 3 1/2 inch diameter fly reel with a contracted width of 1 1/8 inch. It is constructed of cast aluminum with pillars and foot riveted on both sides. Non-adjustable check. A trout reel in good-vg condition from 1951.

"McGill" Autograph Model No. 3B single action fly reel with drag adjustment mounted on the spool. Teardrop lever on reverse alternates tension from left to right hand retrieve. From *Eagle Claw* (Wright & McGill) of Denver, Colorado.

Although unmarked, this *Featherlight* fly reel is made by Meisselbach, and bears an 1896 patent date. The winding knob of this small, nickel plated trout model is painted wood. Counter balance on the spool is solid brass and also plated. This reel is in good-very good condition.

No 150-R Lawrence *Sunbeam* fly reel from Lawrence Tackle Mfg., New York. A clean, stamped metal trout reel in the original box — still very functional, but not worth much as a collectible.

The St. Joe No. 1170 from South Bend Bait Co. Similar in design to the Meisselbach *Featherlight* fly reel, the Shakespeare *Kazoo,* and the Pflueger *Progress.* Made of blued-steel with a simple click drag.

68

(No Model.)

A. F. & W. MEISSELBACH.
FISHING REEL.

No. 553,069.   Patented Jan. 14, 1896.

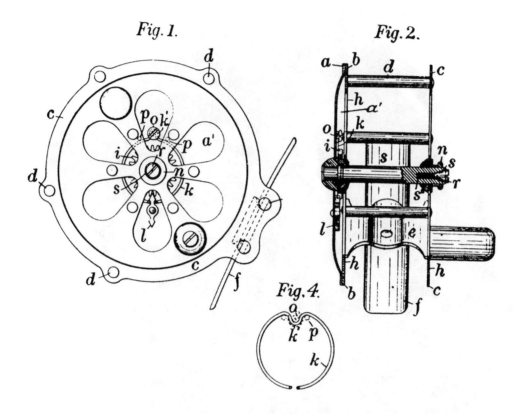

Fig. 1.   *Fig. 2.*

Fig. 4.

August and William Meisselbach of Newark, New Jersey were granted this patent in 1896. The specifications outlined therein provide a detailed description of several important fishing reel improvements designed to eliminate certain problems that the Meisselbach's found in similar reels of the time. They expose one such problem and their solution; . . . *the pivot pin for the click . . . is in all cases riveted to prevent it from being jarred loose in the normal action of the click in engagement with its toothed wheel, and it is therefore impracticable to secure the said click removably in place for convenient renewal. As such member of the device receives the hardest wear and its renewal can be attended only with considerable expense and with the inconvenience of its return to the manufacturer for such purpose, we have devised the double headed click (l), which may be readily reversed so as to double the life of such member by the mere removal of the spring(k) to release the same from its normally radial position.* Note: The spring is removed by means of a single screw(o).

Carlton Mfg. Co. of Rochester, N.Y. *Lightweight* single action fly reel in very good condition. The reel can be easily disassembled by means of a unique pillar to frame connection.

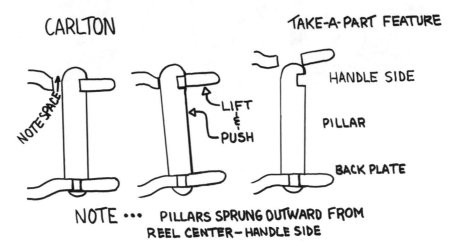

SEQUENCE OF TAKE-A-PART . . . Starting with one of the upper pillars (non-foot area), push to reel center while lifting upper plate. Keep pressure on plate and move to other upper pillar — then push to center. This should release the upper part of the plate. Now release one of the bottom pillars and the plate should be free — if not, try again.

Union Hardware of Torrington, Conn. sold this fly reel around 1930. It is Model No. 7169 with a black painted finish over aluminum. The spool is concave at the face and has an interesting perforation pattern. The winding knob appears to be ivory.

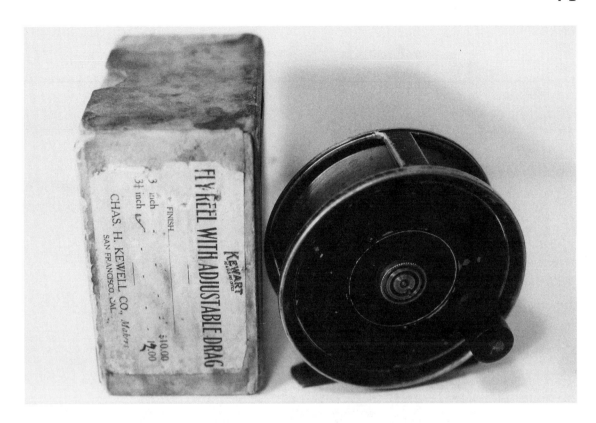

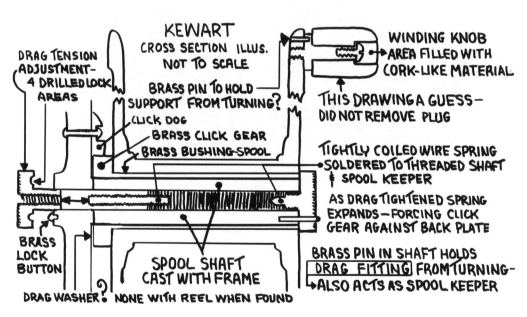

"Kewart" fly reel c.1918, Chas. H. Kewell Co. Makers, San Francisco, CA. Black finish, cast aluminum frame and spool with a brass reel foot. Kewarts are extremely rare, so a value estimate is difficult. Author Jellison's diagram illustrates unique mechanical features of the Kewart.

Duncan Briggs Model #2 fly reel from Providence, RI. 3 1/4 inch size, with a cast aluminum frame. Line guide can be moved for left or right hand retrieve.

73

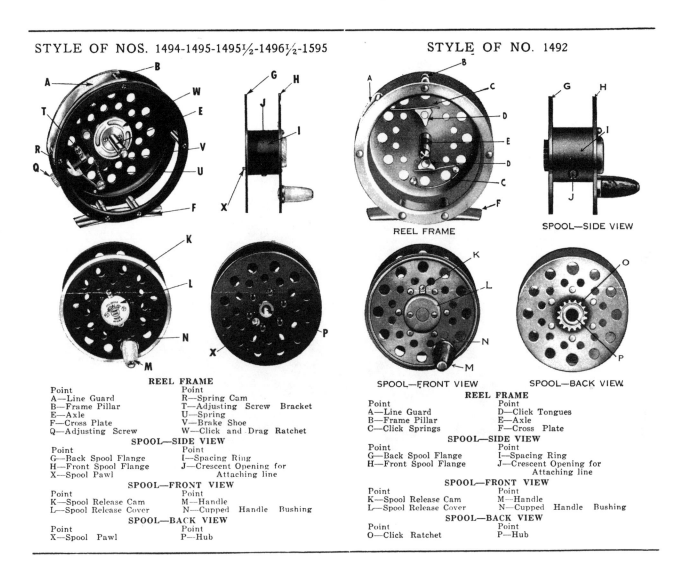

STYLE OF NOS. 1494-1495-1495½-1496½-1595 — STYLE OF NO. 1492

REEL FRAME

Point	Point
A—Line Guard	R—Spring Cam
B—Frame Pillar	T—Adjusting Screw Bracket
E—Axle	U—Spring
F—Cross Plate	V—Brake Shoe
Q—Adjusting Screw	W—Click and Drag Ratchet

SPOOL—SIDE VIEW

Point	Point
G—Back Spool Flange	I—Spacing Ring
H—Front Spool Flange	J—Crescent Opening for Attaching line
X—Spool Pawl	

SPOOL—FRONT VIEW

Point	Point
K—Spool Release Cam	M—Handle
L—Spool Release Cover	N—Cupped Handle Bushing

SPOOL—BACK VIEW

Point	Point
X—Spool Pawl	P—Hub

REEL FRAME

Point	Point
A—Line Guard	D—Click Tongues
B—Frame Pillar	E—Axle
C—Click Springs	F—Cross Plate

SPOOL—SIDE VIEW

Point	Point
G—Back Spool Flange	I—Spacing Ring
H—Front Spool Flange	J—Crescent Opening for Attaching line

SPOOL—FRONT VIEW

Point	Point
K—Spool Release Cam	M—Handle
L—Spool Release Cover	N—Cupped Handle Bushing

SPOOL—BACK VIEW

Point	Point
O—Click Ratchet	P—Hub

A parts chart for the Pflueger Medalist single action fly reels from the 1940-1950 era. Note that the smaller model #1492 is equipped with a non-adjustable check, while the larger models offer a reliable, adjustable drag. Most fly fishers are also familiar with the distinguishable, protracted retrieve-click of the Medalist from model #1494 up.

A Heddon Automatic "Free-Stripping" fly reel, not commonly found in working condition. The reel has a gold finish with white engraved lettering on its face.

A sleek, black *Garcia-Matic* No. 1430 automatic fly reel from the late 1960s, in excellent condition.

The *Kelso* automatic made by H.J. Frost & Co., New York. Patented November, 1907. This is one of the more collectible automatic fly reels. A tough one to grade since the exterior is beat (poor-fair) and the mechanics are good-vg. Would place at the good price due to the age.

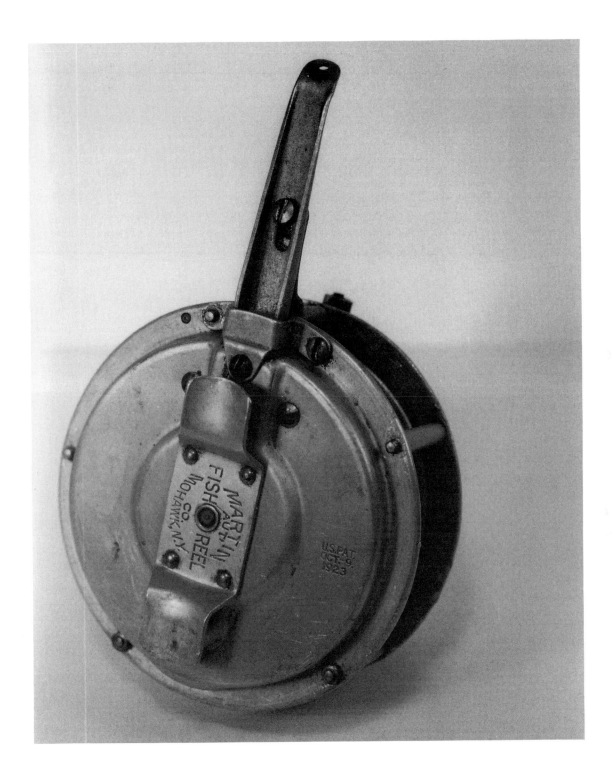

Martin automatic fly reel circa 1930, with the familiar, October 1923 patent date. Most aluminum, spring-loaded automatics are common and have not, as yet, become very valuable — this early *Martin* is no exception.

An unusual, German made DAM (Quick) automatic fly reel with a trout engraved on the face.

J.C. Higgins No 3152 automatic fly reel shown here with the original box and in excellent condition. Again, despite the nostalgic charm and appearance of this circa 1950 automatic, it has very little collectible value.

An older automatic from *South Bend.* The "Orenomatic" Free Stripping Fly Rod Reel. This Model No.1125 is in the original yellow and red box (circa 1930) with attractive graphics. A sturdy, well made automatic in excellent condition.

Yawman & Erbe automatic reel bearing the 1888 and 1891 patents. This is the second of the famous Y&E models, which features a key wind (missing key). Made in Rochester, New York around 1895.

A later model "Y&E" automatic sold by the Horrocks-Ibbotson Company circa 1910. Any Yawman & Erbe reel is highly collectible, but difficult to find in good working order.

OCEAN AND BIG GAME REELS

Ancient Conroy *ball-handle* reel of solid brass made in New York prior to the Civil War. The beautiful winding knob is of turned rosewood. These "New York" style brass reels were handmade from 1840 to 1880. A few were crafted in silver on a special order basis. Another maker from this era was Frederich Vom Hofe (father of famous reel craftsmen Edward and Julius Vom Hofe), who built reels for early tackle houses such as Bradford & Anthony of Boston and Peck & Snyder of New York.

Liberty Bell Company Bristol, Connecticut — Model #250 (A). A scarce reel with a unique free-spool mechanism activated by a slight turn of the winding knob, clockwise. Nickel-plated brass and black bakelite construction. The design of the *Liberty Bell* is attributed to Edward Rockwell, who assigned the patent to the Liberty Bell Co. in 1903.

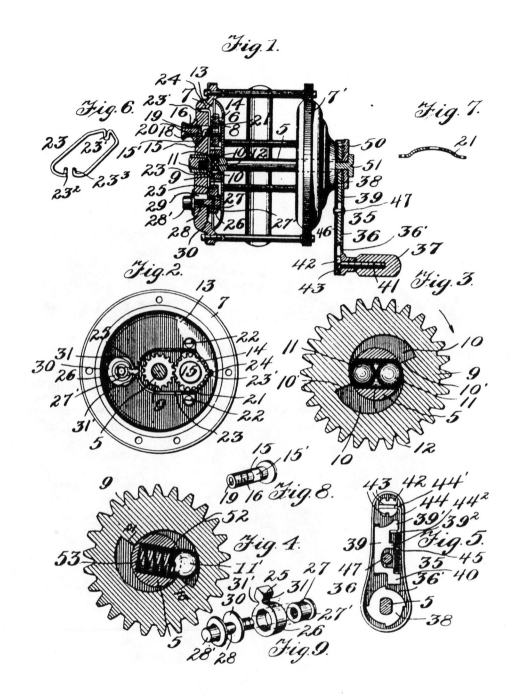

A portion of the complex Rockwell patent of March 31, 1903. Rockwell states that . . . *the brake and click will have no effect upon the reel while winding the line, but will instantly be brought into use when said line is pulled out should a* **strike** *have been made. A further object of the invention is the provision of a fishing reel having a handle so constructed that the reel may rotate free of said handle while the line is being drawn out, but will be automatically connected thereto when it is turned to wind in the line.*

Ocean City *Fortescue,* 250 yard capacity, quality ocean reel with free-spool clutch, made in Philadelphia about 1935. This is probably Ocean City's most attractive salt water fishing reel, constructed almost entirely of German silver — with a fancy wood winding knob. Features a star tension washer for drag or free-spool adjustment on the back plate. Similar to the Ocean City *Sea Girt* (a plated reel).

Ocean City *Sylph* bay reel made of very lightweight aluminum. Although this model has a cheap appearance, it is sturdy and quite functional.

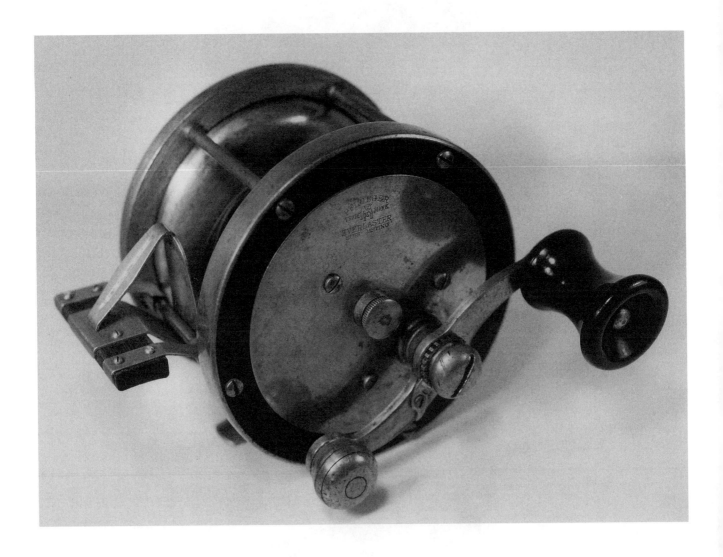

Pflueger *Everlaster* surf casting reel made of hard rubber and plated brass. The example shown is equipped with a *Gem Wood Thumb Brake* in the 2 1/8" size. The Gem brake patent is dated May 31, 1921.

The Pflueger *Norka* salt water mooching reel equipped with a sturdy level-wind mechanism and free spool clutch. Heavy nickel-plated brass finish. A mainstay for salmon fishing in the Pacific Northwest (c.1950).

Pflueger *Golden West* salt water bay reel (older "patented" logo). The reel shown would be in good-very good condition had a previous owner not botched the foot with a rasp. This model is not to be confused with the Pflueger *Golden West Fly Reel* worth considerably more.

Pflueger *Templar* Model 1420 1/2, a deep sea big game reel featuring an adjustable star-drag and free-spool clutch. The reel measures to about a 6/0 size, but is extra wide for greater line capacity.

A close-up of the famed Pflueger-Williams patented drag, which could be added as an aftermarket replacement handle assembly. Used extensively on ocean reels like the *Pflueger Alpine*. Unlike earlier handle drags, the Williams design allowed for adjustment in-between casts or while fighting a fish—without the use of a screw driver or special tool.

Pflueger *Capitol* No. 1988, a heavy ocean trolling reel. It possesses a star-drag and distinguished, square push-button free-spool mechanism. The winding knob is marbled plastic. Pflueger brand wrench also shown.

Capitol
No. 1785-1788
(Discontinued)

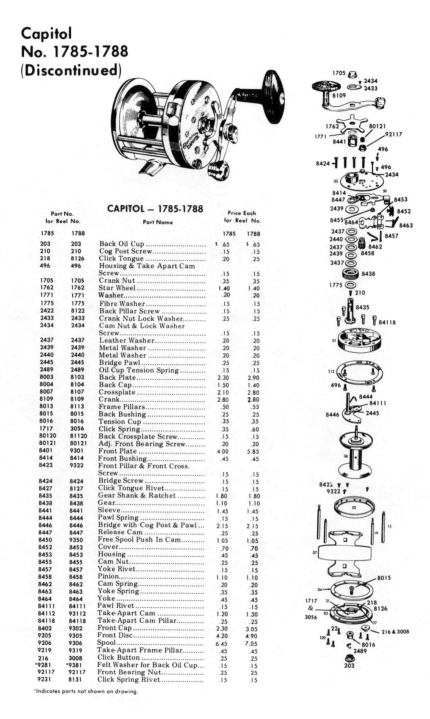

CAPITOL — 1785-1788

Part No. for Reel No. 1785	Part No. for Reel No. 1788	Part Name	Price Each for Reel No. 1785	Price Each for Reel No. 1788
203	203	Back Oil Cup	$ .65	$ .65
210	210	Cog Post Screw	.15	.15
218	8126	Click Tongue	.20	.25
496	496	Housing & Take Apart Cam Screw	.15	.15
1705	1705	Crank Nut	.35	.35
1762	1762	Star Wheel	1.40	1.40
1771	1771	Washer	.20	.20
1775	1775	Fibre Washer	.15	.15
2422	8122	Back Pillar Screw	.15	.15
2433	2433	Crank Nut Lock Washer	.25	.25
2434	2434	Cam Nut & Lock Washer Screw	.15	.15
2437	2437	Leather Washer	.20	.20
2439	2439	Metal Washer	.20	.20
2440	2440	Metal Washer	.20	.20
2445	2445	Bridge Pawl	.25	.25
2489	2489	Oil Cup Tension Spring	.15	.15
8003	8103	Back Plate	2.30	2.90
8004	8104	Back Cap	1.50	1.40
8007	8107	Crossplate	2.10	2.80
8109	8109	Crank	2.80	2.80
8013	8113	Frame Pillars	.50	.55
8015	8015	Back Bushing	.25	.25
8016	8016	Tension Cup	.35	.35
1717	3056	Click Spring	.35	.60
80120	81120	Back Crossplate Screw	.15	.15
80121	80121	Adj. Front Bearing Screw	.20	.20
8401	9301	Front Plate	4.00	5.85
8414	8414	Front Bushing	.45	.45
8422	9322	Front Pillar & Front Cross. Screw	.15	.15
8424	8424	Bridge Screw	.15	.15
8427	8127	Click Tongue Rivet	.15	.15
8435	8435	Gear Shank & Ratchet	1.80	1.80
8438	8438	Gear	1.10	1.10
8441	8441	Sleeve	1.45	1.45
8444	8444	Pawl Spring	.15	.15
8446	8446	Bridge with Cog Post & Pawl	2.15	2.15
8447	8447	Release Cam	.25	.25
8450	9350	Free Spool Push In Cam	1.05	1.05
8452	8452	Cover	.70	.70
8453	8453	Housing	.45	.45
8455	8455	Cam Nut	.25	.25
8457	8457	Yoke Rivet	.15	.15
8458	8458	Pinion	1.10	1.10
8462	8462	Cam Spring	.20	.20
8463	8463	Yoke Spring	.35	.35
8464	8464	Yoke	.45	.45
84111	84111	Pawl Rivet	.15	.15
84112	93112	Take-Apart Cam	1.20	1.30
84118	84118	Take-Apart Cam Pillar	.25	.25
8402	9302	Front Cap	2.30	3.05
9205	9305	Front Disc	4.20	4.90
9206	9306	Spool	6.45	7.05
9219	9319	Take-Apart Frame Pillar	.45	.45
216	3008	Click Button	.25	.25
*9281	*9381	Felt Washer for Back Oil Cup	.15	.15
92117	92117	Front Bearing Nut	.25	.25
9231	8131	Click Spring Rivet	.15	.15

*Indicates parts not shown on drawing.

Reel repair shops and anglers were provided with repair manuals so parts could be conveniently and efficiently ordered. This is a page from the 1969 manual giving a breakdown of the Pflueger Capitol No. 1786-1788 reels. By the late 1960s these models had been discontinued, but Pflueger was still able to provide replacement parts.

Four Brothers *Pontiac* Model #357, blued-brass bay reel. Pflueger and Four Brothers were among several trade names for the Enterprise Manufacturing Company of Akron, Ohio. Consequently, this reel is similar to the Pflueger made *Sumco* (Model #2258), *Temco, Pontiac Surfcasting,* and *Mohawk* reels. Some of these reels could also be found in a nickel-plated finish.

300 yard "Crown" Fishing Tackle Works, Philadelphia—compact trolling reel believed to be built by Montague circa 1922. Nickel-plated construction 3 1/4 inches in diameter and 2 3/8 inches wide. Similar construction to the 200 yard *Winchester* #2744 reel, with the exception of riveted pillars on the front plate of the Winchester.

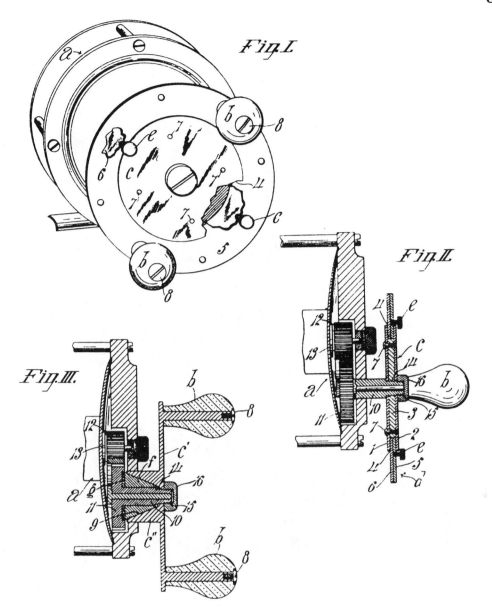

The Francis Rabbeth crank-handle drag assembly as shown in the original 1902 patent application. Clearly, Rabbeth was a very practical man. He succinctly writes . . . *the objects of this invention are to provide improved means for playing the fish and preventing it from getting slack line, to avoid danger of injury to the hand of the fisherman when the fish makes his rushes, and to make provision for paying out the line in such a way as to absolutely prevent the breakage of tackle.* Of course, Rabbeth's creation would not totally eliminate busted knuckles because the angler still had to quickly and firmly grab the crank knob to utilize the drag. Years later, Pflueger sold a similar handle drag, called the "Cub" — a popular add-on accessory for smaller reels such as the Supreme.

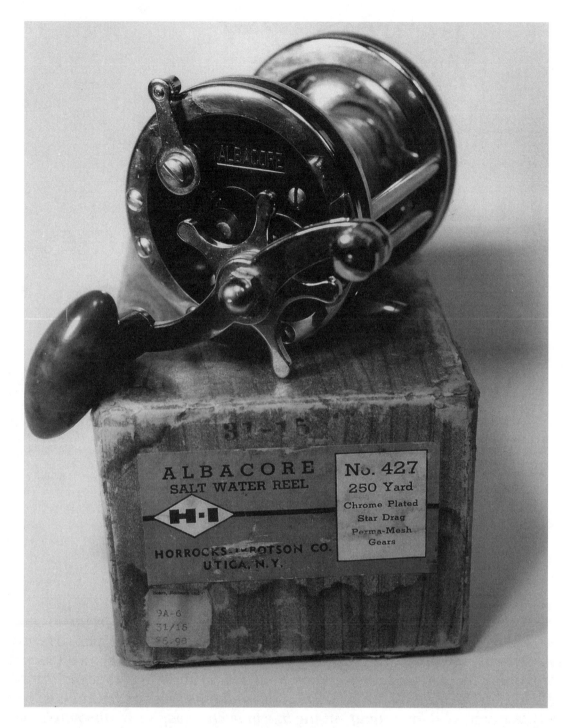

Horrocks-Ibbotson of Utica, New York marketed this salt water trolling reel *Albacore*, named after the long-fin tuna pursued in the late summer off the west coast from Mexico to Washington State. It is Model #427 equipped with a "washer sandwich" type star drag assembly and a molded-plastic torpedo handle—a reel style popular in the 1970s.

The back plate of a Shakespeare *Jupiter* No.2213 salt water bay reel. This was a high quality reel made of nickel-silver and fashioned with a turned wood knob. Shakespeare incorporated a free-spool clutch into the simple, but sturdy design (c.1935). Noticeable finish wear brings the condition grade of this reel down to the very good level.

Early Penn #15 ocean reel (c.1940). A 250 yard line capacity model of hard plastic, exhibiting a wood winding knob. This older Penn has not been fished much and is in excellent condition with the exception of some wear to the screw heads.

A *Freespool* 100 yard reel apparently produced by Montague in the late 1920s. This outstanding, German silver, bay or light casting reel displays twin wood crank knobs mounted to an elegant, long handle. A star washer tension adjustment is located on the back plate.

A basic Julius Vom Hofe bay reel with 1889 patent date engraved on its face. The winding crank knob is shaped, hard rubber and reel construction is nickel plated brass. Notice the pitting and flaking of the nickel (a cosmetic flaw caused by improper storage) which detracts from the great mechanical condition of this example. A tough reel to grade. The authors might place it at the very good level—with the price ranging toward the excellent amount, since older reels in perfect mechanical order are becoming more difficult to find.

Edward Vom Hofe #621 big game reel made in New York. This is the 6/0 size. Constructed of German silver and hard rubber. Equipped with the early, perforated, adjustable star drag. The familiar May 20, 1902 patent date is present and engraved on the silver front oil cap. Silver, off-set foot is longer in front. What a beautiful piece of craftsmanship! An absolute joy to take-apart and work on.

No. 700,424.   Patented May 20, 1902.

E. VOM HOFE.
FISHING REEL.
Application filed Jan. 9, 1902.

(No Model.)

FIG. 1.   FIG. 2.

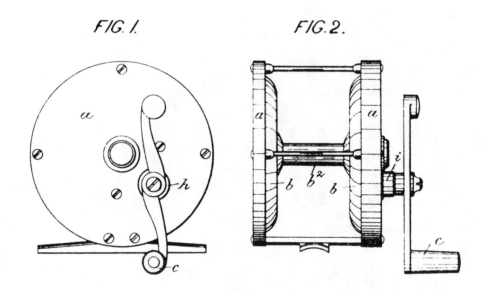

The Edward Vom Hofe Patent of May 20, 1902. Vom Hofe's design is considered to be, essentially, the first "Star Drag" mechanism—although a "star" adjustment device was not included in this patent and it does not yet incorporate an anti-reverse function. Here, by turning a nut on the shaft (part i — *figure 2*) tension of the internal brake is adjusted. It is not hard to follow the master reel maker's rational . . . *This invention relates to a fishing reel of the class in which a friction-brake is interposed between the handle and the spool, so that the line can be run out under tension by the fish, while the handle is held in a fixed position. In this way the line need not be reeled out constantly while the fish is hooked, overrunning and fouling of the line are prevented, and any injury to the hand, owing to a violent jerk on the line, is avoided.*

SPINNING (FIXED SPOOL) REELS

An Orvis Model 150(A) light spinning reel made in Italy. The famous mail order house marketed these excellent fixed spool reels in several sizes from ultra-light to saltwater. This example has a black enamel finish and was produced during the 1960s. Orvis advertised that this series of spinning reels was designed by Fiat (the car company) engineers.

A *Zebco Cardinal* 3. This Swedish made ultra-light spinning reel is green and off-white in color, and is fitted with *Teflon* gears. In the opinion of the authors, it has the finest, most adjustable drag of any fixed spool reel ever produced. These models are highly prized by anglers and still fished all over the world.

Mitchell 300 spinning reel. This early model has the classic, half-bail and all-metal winding knob. Original, French made Mitchells are getting harder to find in the better condition ranges and are popular with spinning reel enthusiasts. Their value, relative to other collectible reels, is low. Many of the early Mitchells and Garcia-Mitchells are still fished.

Shakespeare marketed this American made Model #2000 medium spinning reel in 1975. Author Jellison received it for repair, at that time, with the complaint that it was hard to retrieve line with the drag set under any pressure. The problem remains unsolved to this day.

A red, Penguin brand model 100 fixed spool reel from the 1950s. These inexpensive spinning reels were made of heavy, cast metal with simple, but serviceable, sandwich type drag washer assemblies.

The Pflueger *Sea Star* spinning reel (Model 1050) in excellent condition, a rarity for larger reels of this type. Most big, saltwater spinning reels received heavy abuse from the strain of the game fish, and the harsh elements. The handle and reel foot assembly break-down for storage.

Pflueger's best fresh water spinning reel was the *Pelican* pictured above. This is a Model 1020 (Patent Pending). The unique aspect to the design of this reel is the collapsible foot for compact storage in a tackle box.

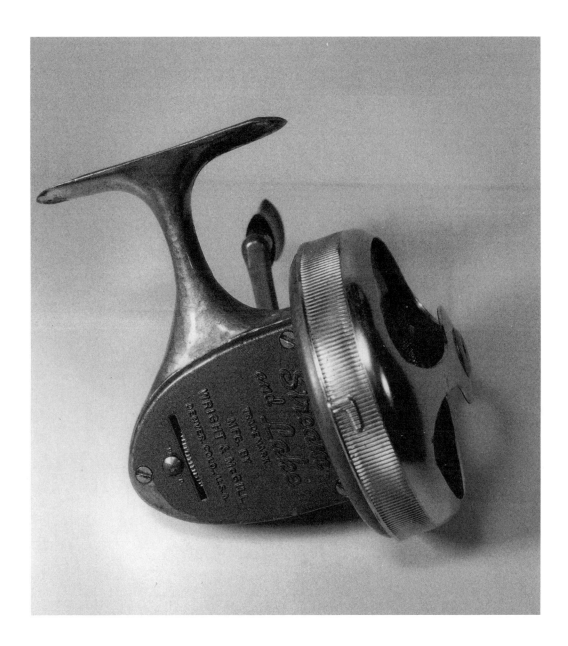

Looking much like a UFO, this Wright & McGill *Stream and Lake* spinning reel is rather unusual. It possesses a convenient, adjustable drag which is evident at the rear of the gear housing. Produced circa 1950 in Denver, Colorado.

A Bache Brown *Mastereel-Spinster* (Catalog No.813) made by the Airex division of Lionel Corporation. This is a Model 3 with the finger bail and collapsible handle. An interesting feature is its anti-reverse lock control built into the handle crank-shaft.

Martin *Precision* spinning reel from Mohawk, New York. The gear housing cover is transparent, revealing the entire mechanism. Identical to the opaque bodied Martin #27 *Precision* spinning reel.

Shakespeare *Wondercast* #1775 spin casting reel, new in the original box.
This Wondercast is about as good as old spin casting reels get. A very fine
drag adjustment is operated by rotating the aluminum spool cover left(lighter)
or right(stronger). A quality, serviceable reel that can be fished, and should
not cost a lot of dough.

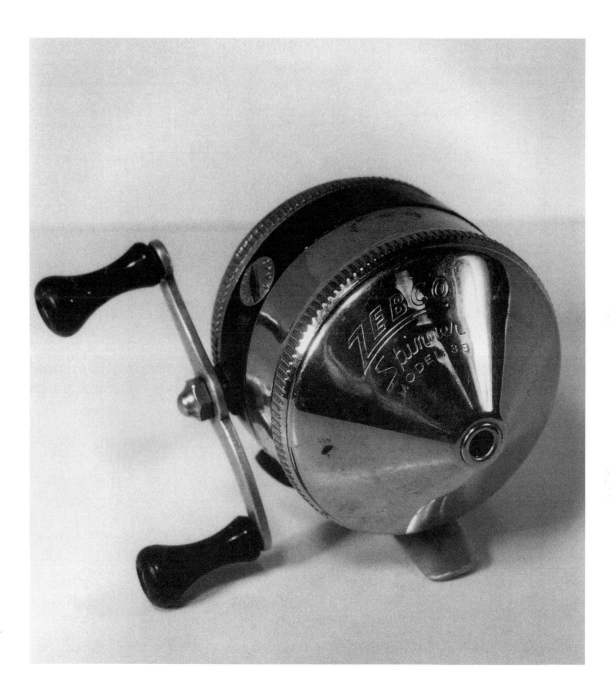

A Zebco 33 spin casting reel from the 1950s. The Zebco 33 has stood the test of time, as evidenced by the number of these reels still in use today. It is nearly impossible to visit a dock, pier or river bank where this mass produced classic has not helped capture a big stringer of fish.

A Wright & McGill "Fre-Line" spin casting type reel, new in the original box. Made in Denver, Colorado circa 1960. An oddity, but not worth much to veteran collectors.

Humphreys Model 4(A) stainless steel spin-cast type reel made in Denver, Colorado about 1952. A push with the thumb on the flat release lever, pops-out the spool—leaving the line to flow freely from the center hole.

SPECIALTY (UNUSUAL) REELS

The Heddon *Winona* was a very popular steelhead reel during the 1940s and 50s. This example, in the original early box, is complete with click indicator, line guide, and leather brake pad. These devices were often removed by eccentric old timers—beware! In the Northwest, according to author Jellison, there was no happy medium . . . *The Winona was either sworn by or sworn at.*

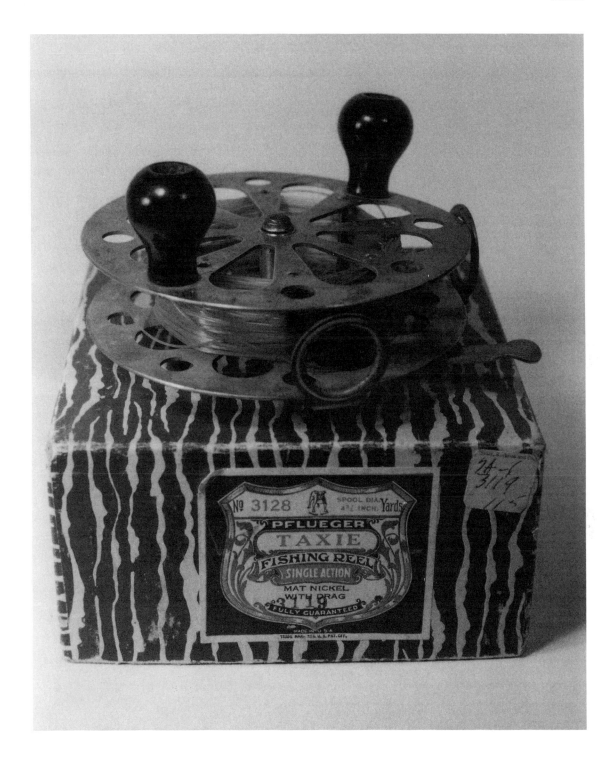

A nickel plated Pflueger *Taxie* trolling reel with manual lever drag and wood winding knobs. This model, No.3128, was made in December, 1936 and is shown with the original box. It was designed to mount flat on the rod. List price was only one dollar and sixty-five cents.

Pflueger *Pakron* trolling reel, later Model No.3178. A 1941 Pflueger catalog lists an earlier Model No. 3180 that is similar in appearance and designed especially for lake trout fishing with wire line. Holds 1200 feet of 20 gauge copper wire.

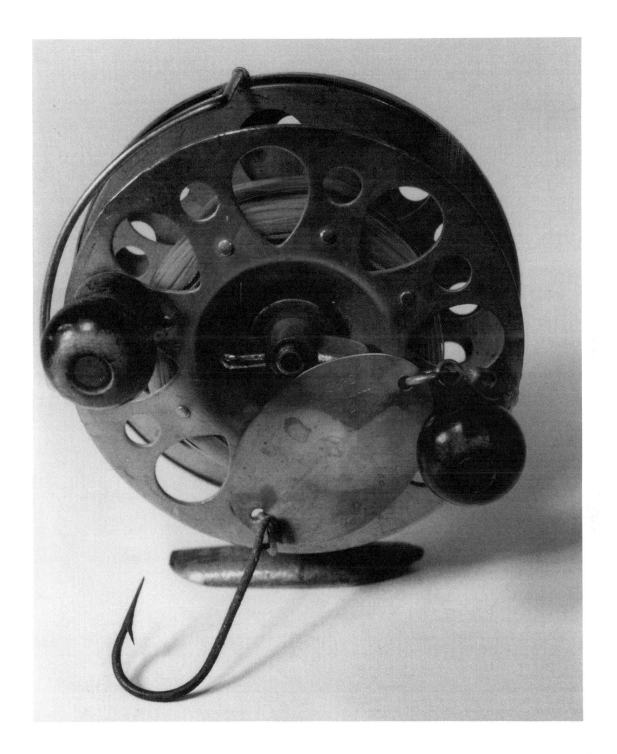

A "Jubilee 4 1/2 Deep Trolling Reel" made by the Gibbs Tool Works of Vancouver, British Columbia. This is a heavy, nickel-plated reel with dual wood winding knobs and a wire line guide. (*Gibbs Egg Wobbler # 1* spoon is also shown).

The *Hermos Brand* trolling reel from 1920. The frame design is curiously similar to the *Meisselbach Expert* single action fly reel—having a flexible, one piece drum. Construction is nickel plated brass with a wood knob and counterbalance mounted on the spool. Pressure on the reel frame from the angler's thumb would flex the frame against the edge of the spool for a crude "drag" operation.

Worden's "Belt Reel" was strapped to the fisherman's belly, not mounted on the rod. It was made by Yakima Bait Company of Granger, Washington. This one was used with a greased silk fly line for fishing large salmon rivers.

The *Magic Fishing Reel* from Denver, Colorado. Each was well made, with a serial number engraved at the side plate. Winding crank knobs are a colorful, marbled plastic. "Magics" are desirable and rather strange contraptions that are widely sought by collectors.

Hardy Brothers' *Silex* No.2 — sometimes called a "spinning reel", was actually used to cast heavy natural baits or artificial lures by means of a revolving, perforated spool and integrated brake system. Popular to this day with Canadians for casting big floats while steelhead drift fishing.

A "Keen Kaster No. 6" made in Bellingham, WA. This model is almost identical to the later Keen Kasters built by *Ravenna Metal Products* in Seattle, Washington. Why was the Keen Kaster special? It was noticeably unattractive. It had very few parts. And it was cheap. Now there's the rub — pure simplicity! Keen Kasters are the invention of Charles O'Hara and William Quirt, who unequivocally state in the original patent . . . *It has also been found that the manual braking means described is all that is needed to make this simple form of reel quite as useful as the more complex braking mechanism required in the ordinary reel. There are no hidden and delicate parts in our reel to become clogged and injured by the presence of sand in its mechanism as quite often happens when using the well known form* (October 29, 1928).

The reel at top is another version of the "Keen Kaster" made in Bellingham, WA. Pictured below it are three earlier *Keen Kasters*, some with Patent Pending markings (circa 1928-1935). All hail from Bellingham and are constructed of aluminum, with different perforation patterns in the drum so as to prevent mildew and line rot.

Peetz Tackle LTD of Victoria, British Columbia made this wood trolling reel exhibiting black winding knobs and attractive brass fittings. Peetz reels are often mistaken for older British antiques (such as the 19th century *Nottingham* wood reels), so be careful—these neat looking, high quality Peetz reels are still being produced and most are **not very old.**

A genuine English *Nottingham* style wood reel, with solid mahogany drum and a brass cross brace or so-called "star back" design. The long reel foot is incorporated into the back brace and extends directly therefrom. Many of these beautiful reels made of mahogany or walnut were sold from 1880 to 1920. Some were produced with a revolving lineguide, adjustable tension drag, perforated spool, horn knobs, ivory knobs, or fancy fittings.

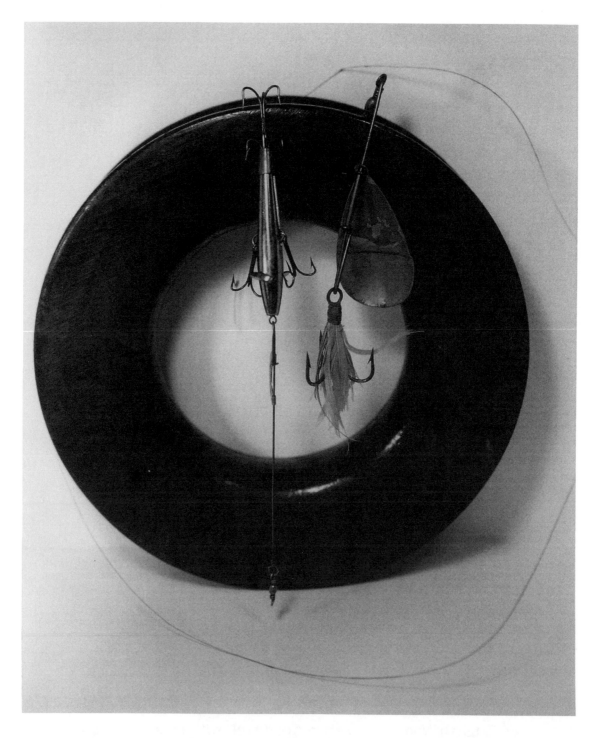

The maker of this reel most surely created the epitome of simplicity. No handle, no reel foot, no gears, and no connection to a rod. And the fish didn't know the difference! This artistically shaped hand-line reel is turned of solid mahogany. It was used, very effectively, off the piers and docks of Southern Florida.

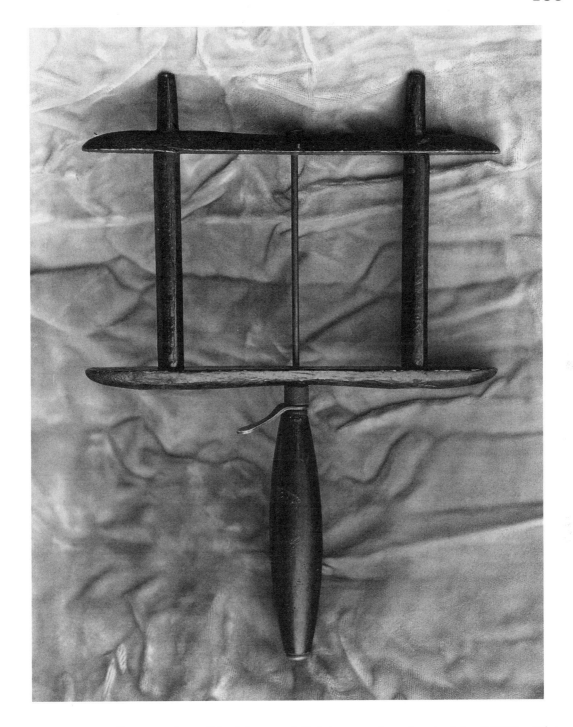

The Earnest Pflueger *hand-held wood fishing reel,* patented in 1896. This example is painted black. The authors have seen the same reel in green and yellow as well. This scarce "reel" lingered for years in author Jellison's basement—he thought it was an old kite flyer or fly line dryer. At present, the Pflueger wood reel is tough to price because very few have been offered for sale as collectible fishing reels!

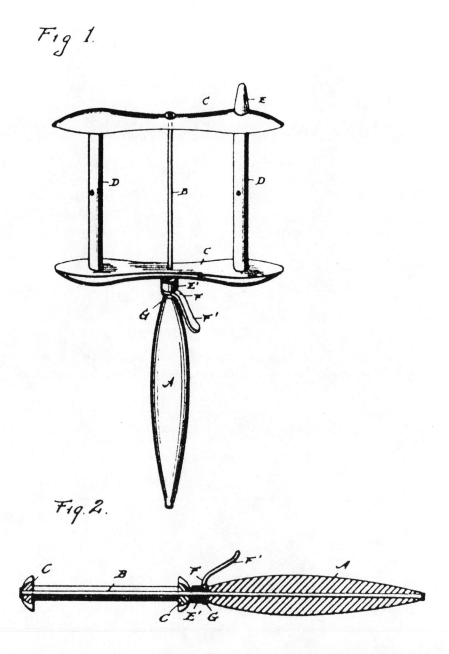

Fig 1.

Fig. 2.

Earnest Pflueger of Akron, Ohio filed his patent application for the hand held wood reel on December 27, 1895. A patent (No.560,925) was granted five months later. Pflueger describes the reel's operation . . . *By depressing the handle of the lever the cushion* **E** *is forced against the lower head to check the movement of the reel or bring it to a stop at the will of the holder. The line can be wound up with great rapidity by the use of this reel, which offers the same advantages as other and more expensive reels for playing the fish through the slight holding of the lever to let the reel drag. A further advantage of this reel is that <u>it allows the line to dry readily thereon.</u>*

Huge 6" punched brass trolling reel, homemade and bolted to a steel rod. The crude sliding line guide is integrated into the reel foot. A rotten handle extends out a full three inches. This outfit gives the comical appearance of a heavy duty ice fishing rig. Hundreds of homemade reels are discovered each year by collectors seeking the special and unusual.

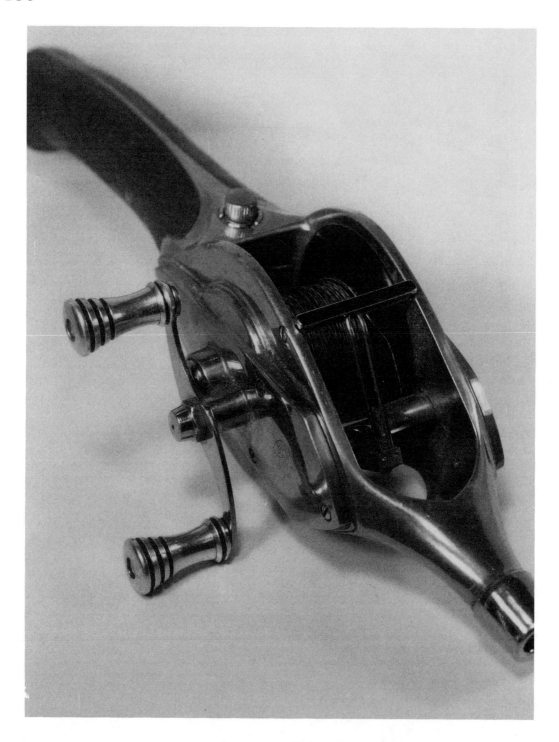

Rods with built in reels are very collectible as exemplified by the *Hurd Super Caster* above. The rod handle is checkered walnut and attaches to a solid steel shaft. Reel is a level-wind style with thumb operated, push-button "drag" behind the spool. A fine *Hurd*, like this one, in excellent condition with the original vinyl case—is worth several hundred dollars.

CARE OF OLD FISHING REELS

Upon discovery, the ideal collectible will be in perfect, clean condition. Unfortunately this "ideal" is not the norm. The bulk of old fishing tackle found by collectors is uncovered in a dark, dusty garage, barn or attic. Often, old reels are dirty. Cleaning a collectible reel is a job relished by few, although several collector-anglers we know actually like to clean and tinker with their new found toys. In any case, the question is always . . . to clean or not to clean? If the answer is "to clean", the following tips may be helpful.

CLEANING

Some old reels, especially simple designs like the single action fly reel, will need nothing more than a light oiling and wipe-down with a damp cloth. However, many casting and spinning reels, particularly those with complex gearing, accumulate dirt and grit mixed with old grease which must be cleaned out. The only way to properly accomplish this is to dismantle (take-down) the reel for a thorough cleaning—inside and out.

Lay the parts out on a white cloth placed in the bottom of a serving tray or rectangular aluminum cake pan. The cloth prevents parts from rolling around if the tray is moved. For easier re-assembly, when working with more complicated reels, remember to lay the parts out—**in order**.

Clean any individual metal parts by soaking in a mild solvent or Murphy's oil soap. A discarded toothbrush will help loosen tough grit between gear teeth or in crevices around fittings.

Your safest route with plastic parts (bakelite, ebonite etc.) is to immerse them in a warm bath of soapy water only. Diluted Murphy's works well.

Salt water corrosion, rust, oxidation and other horrid afflictions may be dealt with through more drastic measures—although care must be taken to assure that the remaining plating or natural patina and luster are not removed. This is especially important when dealing with exterior parts such as end plates, handles, foot, or pillars.

Lightly rub the effected "rusty" area with fine to ultra-fine (0000) steel wool or a soft brass wire brush. Carefully work only on the immediate area of the affliction. Do not ever attempt to shine or clean the entire exterior of a reel with steel wool or a brush. These tools or other abrasive type cleaners will form permanent, small scratches in the metal surface—forever lowering the reel's collectible value.

Keep in mind that the drastic measures used to eliminate a rust spot or small area of corrosion are merely the lesser of two evils. When in doubt about treating such an affliction, it is best to leave well enough alone (especially when dealing with a very valuable reel).

RE-ASSEMBLY & LUBRICATION

When all parts are clean, dry them off with a soft, absorbent cotton cloth. Before re-assembly, lubricate moving parts and any threaded screw-holes with light oil. Fly reels may be lubricated with a light grease or Vaseline (since fast, free spool type action is not required). Finally, buff the whole assembled reel with a separate, soft **cotton** cloth. Never use a paper towel to dry collectible reels. The fibers in paper can be abrasive and may form fine scratches in the finish of the reel—that are especially noticeable on reflective surfaces such as front and back plates.

With respect to cleaning, in general, the following maxim is one to remember:

Practice moderation — clean collectible reels only when absolutely necessary!

REMOVING SCREWS FOR TAKE-DOWN

What may appear on the surface to be a simple task, can be a particularly nasty job if the screw is frozen and will not turn. DO NOT FORCE A "FROZEN" SCREW—you will surely distort the screw head or break it off completely.

First, make sure the correct size screwdriver is used. Have a variety of sizes on hand at the work bench. You may need to modify a screwdriver to fit screw slots on some older reels. Carefully grind the driver to <u>completely fill the area of the slot.</u>

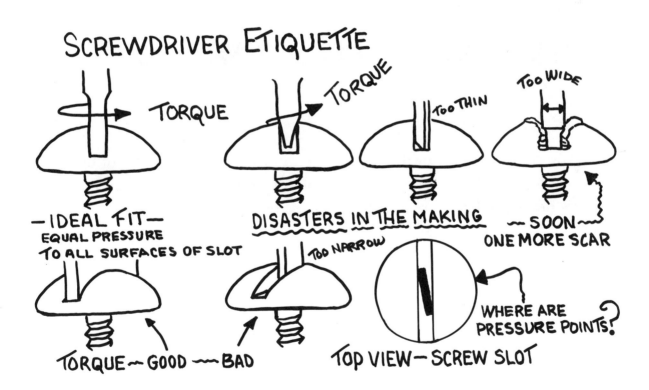

If the correct size screwdriver is used and the screw still will not budge, place a drop of "Liquid Wrench" (or similar break-free type oil) around the screw head and let the reel sit for a day or two.

When ready to proceed:

(1) Lightly tap the top of the screw with a wood mallet or plastic end of the screwdriver.

(2) Gently try to turn a right handed screw to the left.

(3) If no movement, try carefully exerting a little turning pressure to the right to break it free.

(4) Now turn left.

Hopefully you will have successfully dislodged the screw. If not, repeat the procedure.

Caution and patience are the key here. These virtues are a better alternative than trying to hastily remove a frozen screw—and then shearing it off. Removing a sheared-off, headless screw is practically an impossible task (although author Jellison accomplished it a few times—back in the days of his reel repair business!).

NOTE: Sometimes heat can be used to help get the "Liquid Wrench" down into the frozen areas. Obviously, do not use heat near any plastic parts and never use a torch because it will discolor metal. A soldering iron carefully applied on the screw head or pillar (for example), will cause the frozen area to expand and contract—which may help move the Liquid Wrench around.

Finally, be aware that . . . **some screws will never turn** despite all your efforts. If you bought the reel from someone who knew of this problem and did not disclose their knowledge of the defect—you have literally been taken, to put it mildly. But you can take consolation in the fact that most all of us have been hoodwinked once or twice in this hobby!

DEFECTS OR MISSING PARTS
(Ethical Repairs)

Replacing a missing or broken reel part with a genuine, original factory part is considered, by a majority of collectors, to be a legitimate practice. However not all collectors agree on this point because they feel that if the part is not original to <u>that reel</u>, then it is not an original part and therefore downgrades the value of the reel.

It would follow logically that, if we do look upon replacement parts as a legitimate repair option, we must at least require that those parts be from an identical reel of the same age and condition.

Finding factory repair parts for different reel models has been a problem because many of the older reel makers now cease to exist (i.e. there is no "factory" from which to order parts!). Parts that are quickest to wear out become very scarce. Collectors, consequently, look for "parts" reels that can be salvaged and broken down into individual, usable repair parts.

Collectors commonly run into difficulty when, with good intentions, they make a repair with a similar, but **incorrect** part. An example of this could be where a German silver worm gear cover is replaced with a newer chromed piece. Another example that comes to mind involves the most frequently lost and replaced part—a silver, chrome or jeweled bearing end cap. Collectors sometimes place a "non jeweled" cap on a reel that originally sported an agate style cap.

The unscrupulous dealer-repairman might conceivably commit these acts knowing full-well and hoping that *no one will know the difference.* Just remember that there is a *difference* and try to be careful with any legitimate repairs you might undertake. If you should ever sell or trade the reel, it is only fair that the buyer be informed of any repair work or replacement of parts not indigenous to that particular reel.

Heavy repair tasks such as soldering, drilling, welding, pounding, bending, or gluing are most definitely frowned upon by all. Engage in this sort of activity and you could ruin the original integrity of a valuable reel—forever! A poorly maintained, but honorable old reel is worth more in neglected or broken condition than if it were **botched** in a hopeless repair attempt.

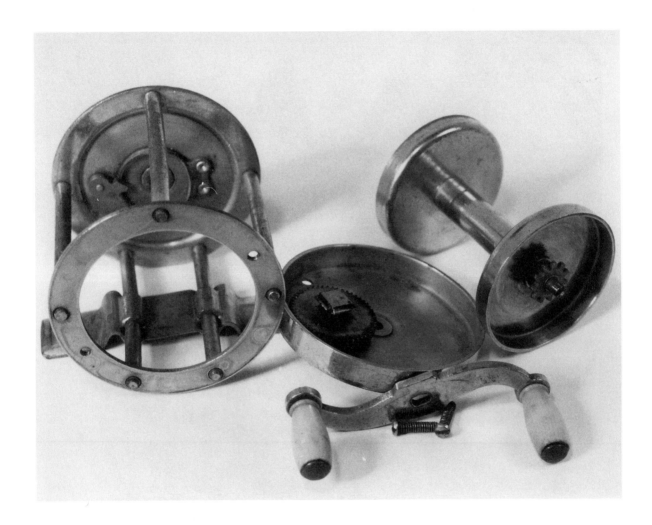

A simple, American made baitcasting reel circa 1910 — taken down for cleaning and repair. Author Jellison dismantled it several years ago and has yet to finish the job! The click ratchet riveted to the back plate is in good working order, so a thorough soaking, wipe down and a bit of grease should be all that is necessary. Occasionally, the spool will rub when first re-assembled. This can often be remedied by loosening and re-tightening screws or working the corrosive (rubbing) areas with a fine brush.

The inside back or "tail" plate of a Meisselbach-Catucci reel, removed by means of the push-button take-a-part feature. Cleaning a complex mechanism such as this is a major undertaking compared to reel on the foregoing page.

A box of Pflueger extra parts that one of the authors keeps on hand for legitimate repairs. Notice the cork arbor with its original label still attached, and the *Little Giant* Pflueger combination screwdriver and wrench (especially made for neatly dismantling and adjusting Pflueger baitcasting reels).

Meisselbach *Rainbow* single action fly reel. Unfortunately the entire spool latch mechanism is missing. The missing device resembles a horseshoe. This is a good example of a reel that can be legitimately repaired — if a correct latch is found. Perhaps an identical reel can be discovered with a broken spool knob but with the <u>latch</u> intact. Who knows? The two worthless, "parts reels" could be combined into a decent, usable whole reel of some value.

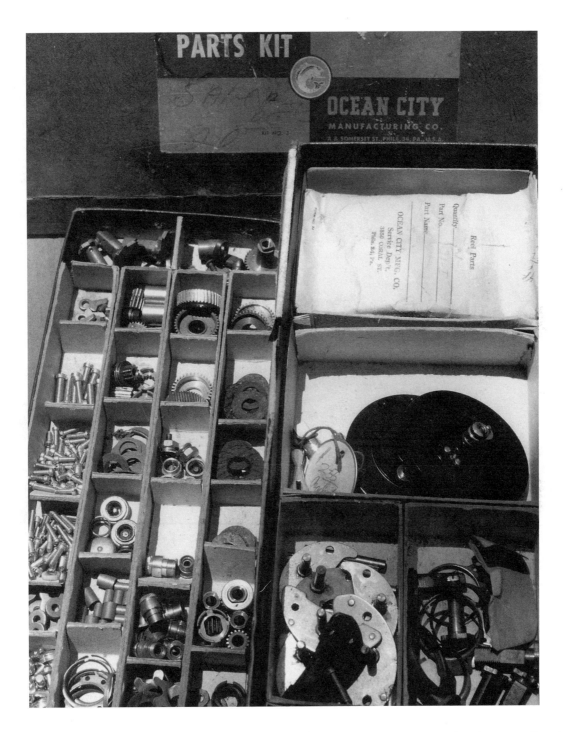

Repair parts kits, like the one pictured above, were an important ingredient to any reel repair business. This Ocean City kit was probably ordered by a tackle shop during the 1940s. Partitioned factory repair boxes are very collectible and useful as well.

Old reels may be found for sale at antique shows, gun shows, and special-ized fishing tackle collectibles shows — where some good deals can be had or you can be had! Do not hesitate to "haggle" with the seller if you think it is justified; this is expected and accepted as common practice. You may spot a defect in a reel that the seller was not aware of, and thus provide bar-gaining leverage to lower the selling price. If the seller is firm on the price, so be it. There is no harm in trying.

FISHING REEL EVALUATION

The value of any collectible or antique is always the subjective view of the possessor. A trained or experienced appraiser, without bias, tends to assign the most objective and accurate estimate of value to a particular piece. However, notwithstanding diligent research into legitimate comparable sales, two independent appraisals of the same object will most certainly yield different results. So, you see, determining the true value of a collectible is far from being an exact science.

Evaluating an old fishing reel is an interesting, yet confusing task for even the most experienced collector. Any reel must be looked at closely, and all factors relating to value must be considered.

When a fishing reel is offered for sale or trade, it is usually accompanied by a grade such as good, very good or excellent (it is surprising how seldom a reel is graded as "poor", though we all know that many poor reels exist!). Individual collectors and organizations have attempted to clarify the grading process, and this is a step in the right direction. For example, The National Fishing Lure Collectors Club has devised a Standard Reel Grading System that takes into account both <u>appearance</u> and <u>mechanical condition</u> on scales of one to ten. Nevertheless, it is the collector or, shall we say with trepidation, part-time dealer who assigns the number "grade" for both appearance and mechanics. Thus, we are back to the subjective factor. Systems like the one above can work satisfactorily if both parties to a sale or trade are familiar with that particular grading process. However, if someone were not aware of the descriptions behind the N.F.L.C.C. system, they might expect much more of a reel described as "Good".

In the formulation of a value guide for this book, we have developed our own simple grading system that can be put to use in assigning values to a particular make and model of reel in three levels of condition. Throughout the length of this book we have attempted to describe and identify various common condition flaws by means of both photograph and narrative. When grading your own reels, it may help to refer back to any applicable photographs in which a reel having similar condition characteristics appears. Try to fairly evaluate each individual reel by matching its condition as closely as possible to one of the "grades" described herein. If it seems to fall "between grades", assign a slightly higher or lower value accordingly.

Our value guidelines take into account current collecting trends, scarcity, and popularity among hobby collectors. The value guide is made to reflects average selling prices in the collectible reel market. This includes comparable sales or reasonable asking prices from antique tackle shows, collector-dealer lists, and tackle auctions. In some cases, trades between two knowledgeable collectors were considered. Prices asked and realized by general dealers in antiques have also been examined, although antique shop prices can be way too high on certain common reels and, on occasion, temptingly low! In any case, our research has identified the general antique dealer as a growing source for tackle collectors, with brisk sales being recorded for dealers who regularly acquire estate tackle and know how to market it. The prices do not take into account purchases at garage sales and flea markets where a good bargain is the rule — and this is as it should be. Regional price variations are used as an indicator of new popularity trends that may cause a certain type of reel to increase in value worldwide. For example; Hardy Silex reels have a strong following in British Columbia. Swedish Ambassadeurs are hot in Japan, and Zebco Cardinal spinning reels command great attention in Kentucky, Ohio, and other parts of the south. Much of the demand is created because the foregoing reels are known for superior function as well as collectible potential.

Hopefully, by combining the information found in this book, along with our grading system and value guidelines — the average collector will be able to adequately appraise his or her favorite reels.

CONDITION

The root to the fair value of any collectibles is its condition. We find the following statements to be true for the most part: (1) Many beginning reel collectors buy almost any old reel they can lay their hands on, regardless of condition. (2) Experienced reel collectors generally look only for those examples in the top grades of condition. Of course, being selective as a beginning buyer is very difficult. A certain amount of "beginner's zeal" adds to the fun, and most reel collectors get started without making too many costly mistakes. In fact, experienced collectors can get too hung-up on perfection and the hobby of reel collecting can then become serious, boring business.

What does this all have to do with "condition"? Well, not much, except that we want to make the following point and offer some monetary advice. Try to use a bit of restraint if you are just getting started in reel collecting. Become a discriminating reel buyer. Look for legitimate, lightly used or well-cared-for reels that you will want to keep in your collection for a long time. On the other hand, fishing reels were made to be used, well used! There is no shame in collecting functional, honestly fished, cosmetically worn reels.   If your intent is not to maximize the value of your collection, and you do not necessarily care about appreciation or investment potential, the foregoing theory of selective buying goes out the window. Buy anything you find appealing—perhaps a reel like the one you fished with as a kid or an unusual model you just want to "tinker" with. And there lies the heart of the matter. Whether you are fussy about condition or not, make a personal choice in defining your collection, and then attempt to become knowledgeable about condition and value so that you will pay only a fair price for what you do buy.

ANALYSIS OF CONDITION

In order to analyze a reels condition for purposes of assigning value (or determining if the asking price is a "rip-off" or bargain) a sharp eye is necessary. It helps to know where to look, so we have outlined the following procedure, including some areas of caution.

(1) ORIGINAL PARTS

First, look to see if the reel has all original parts. The most commonly replaced parts on a fishing reel are screws. If one or more screws appear to be newer, larger or of a different style than others serving the same function (i.e. frame, cover, or foot screws) an immediate flaw can be identified. Unfortunately, when reels are "taken-down" for cleaning or lubrication, these tiny screws are sometimes dropped on the floor or misplaced. Often the screw was lost many years ago, and was replaced by the owner. However, unless an original screw can be found, a missing or obviously mismatched replacement screw can lessen value substantially (an otherwise excellent reel might be lowered to the "poor - fair" condition level as a result).

Crank knobs, end caps, jeweled bearing caps, and reel feet are sometimes replaced, often with crude, obvious substitutes. With end caps or jeweled caps it is easy to spot a replacement in most cases because the number of threads on the outer sleeve upon which the cap is affixed, will be much different than on the cap itself. Also, the back cap may simply not match the front cap. Replaced crank knobs and even entire crank handle assemblies are more difficult to detect. Often the only way to discern originality is with experience or comparison to another reel or reels of the same exact make or model. Reel feet are not so regularly replaced as they are filed or drilled. A replaced reel foot, however, is sometimes difficult to spot unless you are familiar with that particular reel. Filed or drilled feet are fairly obvious. This example leads us into the following section.

(2) STRUCTURAL DEFECTS

Many reels, especially fly reels, have had their feet filed to allow for use on a rod with a reel seat of inadequate proportion to accommodate that reel. Sadly, collectors frequently come across outstanding reels with but one flaw —a badly filed foot. The reel may be excellent in every way, but due to this horrible disfigurement it can only be considered in fair condition for collecting purposes. For the angler wanting a classic fly reel for actual fishing (Older Hardy reels with brass feet can often be found "filed") a good bargain might be struck, since a moderately filed foot will not effect performance.

Probably more important is the structural defect of a crack or fracture. Cracks are sometimes found on the reel end plates, particularly the back plate of bakelite reels (designated as a back "cover" on older patent drawings) . For example, the beautiful ocean reels of Edward Vom Hofe must be looked at closely for just this type of problem. Cracks can be found where a screw enters the bakelite material or where the reel was hit from a fall. Many old British fly reels were constructed of a soft, cast aluminum alloy that tends to chip or fracture. Defects such as this not only jeopardize the reels structural (and mechanical) integrity, but are very displeasing to the eye.

Fine age cracks often appear in old bone or horn crank knobs. These materials dry out and become brittle. If the cracks are severe, the knob may one day fall apart in your hands. If the cracks are just on the surface, there is little to worry about.

(3) MECHANICAL FUNCTION

If a reel does not function properly, both collectible and practical fishing value are lost. Operate the reel and check all functions to see that they work correctly and smoothly. Functions may include turn of the handle, spool rotation, drag operation and adjustment, take-down features, anti-reverse, and free spool performance to name a few. Older reels, especially those with continuous clicks, sliding-button clicks and drag springs can often be repaired if not functional at first blush. Sometimes a good cleaning and careful tinkering can remedy a non-operating click or drag spring.

A common problem with the older, simple crank reels is that of a non-

154

aligned or bent spool. A bent frame or pillar may be the actual cause of a jerky operation. If the spool does not turn freely, a good cleaning and lubrication may be in order, however the repair may require some careful manipulation of the spool flange, spool shaft, or reel frame. To embark on this sort of procedure could culminate in disaster and may ultimately lower the value even more (obvious tinkering, tool scratches, stripped screws, or fouled screw heads take their toll).

In any event, a high degree of impairment in mechanical function can cause an otherwise clean, original reel to be dropped from one of the higher condition grades to that of poor. Don't count on being able to fix a mechanical problem! Most experienced collectors find it best to assume the worst when deciding what to pay for a reel that falls into this area of caution.

(4) COSMETIC APPEARANCE

It is the pleasing cosmetic appearance of a reel that might first grab the collector's attention. However it can be a mistake to become so enamored with a particular reel that one overlooks more subtle cosmetic flaws. For example, a gleaming appearance can alert the careful buyer to excessive cleaning. Make a close inspection for fine scratches from steel wool or abrasive cleaners. Harsh chemicals and coarse abrasives can remove the original patina that an old reel acquires with age, and reduce collectible value. Deeper scratches from cleaning cause irreparable harm to metal and hard rubber surfaces. Many nickel-plated reels are rendered bare, down to the brass ... so be sure the nice brass reel you are about to purchase was not subjected to this type of cleaning. Any original finish, whether it be nickel, bronze, bluing, or enamel is best if close to 100% intact. If any is worn-away by use or abused by cleaning, a proportionate reduction in value should be considered.

One common cosmetic flaw was created by good intentions. Frequent maintenance and lubrication in some old reel types required removal of screws to get at the mechanical parts. Often the screwdriver slid out of the screw head, causing a slash or gash in the endplate, handle, or pillar. A deep scratch such as this will drop value substantially, while a slight mark or rub will have little effect unless a high level of condition (such as near-mint) is claimed.

Rust or pitting occurs on many old reels, especially those that have been around salt water. Some rust can be cleaned up, but will never be satisfactorily removed since it is a chemical reaction in the metal. A small patch of rust on the reel back, one pillar, or on the spool will effect value much less than a large area on the front, obliterating the trademark or patent dates.

Dirt or grease, on the other hand, are removable evils. Warm water and a mild oil soap, such as Murphy's, can work wonders on the exterior of a soiled reel. Dirty reels can still call for a slight reduction in value because the labor to clean (and possibly take-down and lubricate) should be considered. Inspect a very dirty reel closely. Under all that old dirt may be a rose ... or a skunk!

GRADING SYSTEM

MINT CONDITION - Never been used. May show slight signs of handling. Value enhanced or affirmed if the reel is found in the original box and/or case. Condition of the box or case is important if extra value is added. Make sure the box or case is correct for that reel. "Near mint" is a favorite expression of collectors, but it is often only wishful thinking so we will not use the term here.

EXCELLENT CONDITION - A reel exhibiting very minimal cosmetic wear. Lightly used and mechanically perfect. If accompanied by a clean original box or case, the value will be enhanced.

VERY GOOD CONDITION - A reel with evidence of average use, cosmetic wear, and aging but with no unsightly flaws. Solid mechanically with no defects in structure or performance.

GOOD CONDITION - Reels at this level are well used, but all original parts remain. Possibly deeper scratches or pitting in metal parts. Some mechanical wear, however still fully functional, with no major structural defects. Decent appearance.

FAIR CONDITION - Usually a poor reel with some appealing quality such as; antique appearance, nice patina, size (very small), having a verified provenance or subjective sentimental value. Nevertheless, cannot be graded as "Good" due to major structural, cosmetic or mechanical defects. Value is essentially the same as "poor", but may be higher if the reel is extremely old, rare, or unique.

POOR CONDITION - A reel that is broken, missing parts or graced with non-original parts. On occasion, a complete and functional reel is encountered with such a horrendous cosmetic appearance so as to drop it into the "poor category". Poor and fair reels do retain some value as repair parts, although it is usually only a fraction of the "very good" price.

Antique, handmade brass reels, such as the one pictured above, are valuable despite the presence of deep nicks and scratches. Considering its age of 150 years, this reel is in good-very good condition.

Montgomery Ward *SportKing* brand level-wind casting reel from 1955. Displays an interesting, but not particularly artistic engraved back plate. Notice that the foot has become detached — a major defect that renders an already cheap reel practically worthless.

A great example of a reel back plate with the wrong size, incorrect replacement screw. The screw head is also "botched". Notice the homemade, leather thumber (not original) and substantial pitting of the nickel finished metal on this small bay reel (probably distributed by Pennel around 1925). All of these factors contribute to a condition rating of poor-fair.

On the Left is a nice Hardy St. George fly reel with one glaring flaw — a cracked agate lineguide. It is true that the agate ring can be replaced with a costly repair, however most fly fishers would find this St. George to still be functional <u>as is</u>. The value would be assessed at the good-vg level or less, due to this defect. **On the right** is an early William Shakespeare Jr. *Universal* non level-wind baitcasting reel. A noticeable defect in this reel is the fractured celluloid crank knob on the counter-balanced handle. Cracks and splits like the one shown here are common, especially when the knob is produced of ivory, bone or animal horn. So long as the crack does not run the length of the knob and does not jeopardize structural integrity, it is usually acceptable to collectors and will not substantially downgrade a reel's value.

A pair of Pflueger *Medalist* single action fly reels with their spools removed. The first reel is not only missing the round drag assembly, but also the tension adjustment spring and several screws. From the outside, with the spool in place, the reel looks OK though it does not function properly. Always remember to remove the spool of a fly reel to inspect what's inside. The second *Medalist* is well used, as the rim wear would indicate, but the drag tension adjustment mechanism is still in excellent operating condition (a more important consideration).

B.F. Meek and Sons No.3 Bluegrass Kentucky multiplier (c.1895)

Shakespeare Marhoff #1964 Model HF(1935) with anti-backlash device

Abbey & Imbrie trout reel with ring clamp and hooks trademark (c. 1890)

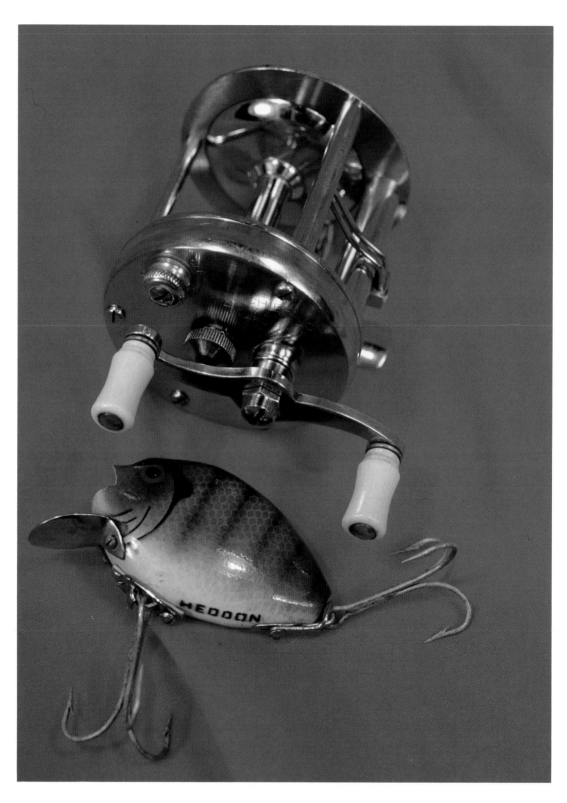

Heddon Chief Dowagiac level-wind multiplying baitcaster (c.1932)

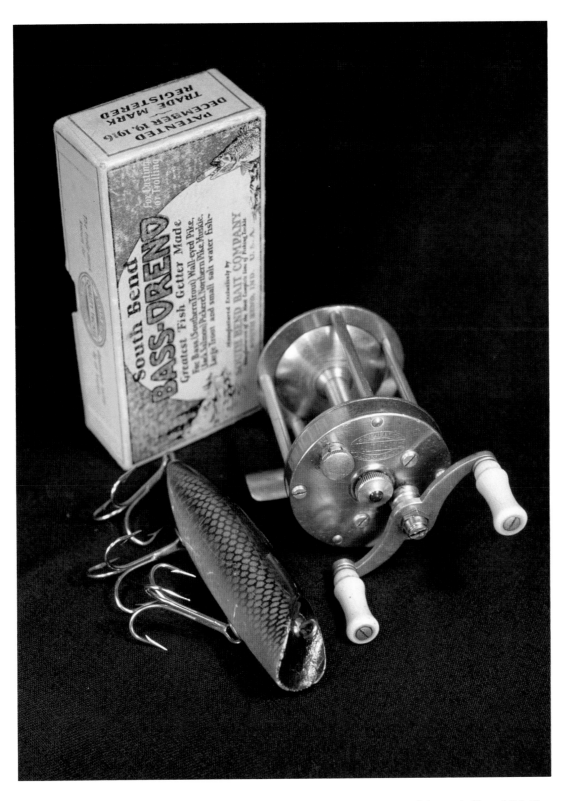

South Bend #1131(A) reel with Bass Oreno bait and box (all c.1916)

A Swedish Ambassadeur 5000C Deluxe (Gold) in the original wood box

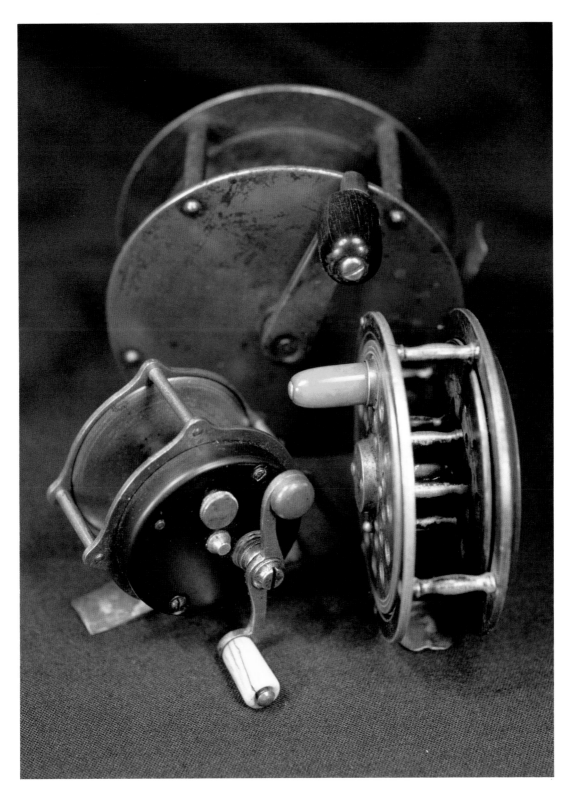

1870 era salmon reel, Julius Vom Hofe trout reel, and early Medalist

Early brass Bronson Go-Getter atop a jeweled Bronson Biltwell #3300

VALUE GUIDE

The following value guide compiled by the authors is, of course, based in part upon research into selling prices for collectible fishing reels in the U.S., Canada, and Europe. However, in the final analysis, all values and values for condition levels are purely the subjective opinion of the authors and derived from averages, trades, reasonable asking prices, trends, and the experienced "hunch". The prices stated are not necessarily a list to determine exactly how much a reel should be sold for or how much one should pay—but rather a rough guideline to help collectors formulate a personal value guide by combining our numbers with those gained from their own experiences.

Remember, no two reels are exactly alike in terms of condition (unless they are "mint" and this highest appraisal of condition is often in dispute) therefore, no two asking prices are exactly alike and may differ greatly due to other factors including:

(1) Who is the seller? For example: Antique shop, gun show dealer, fellow collector, flea market seller, estate sale, general auction, tackle auction.

(2) Motivation of seller. For example: Quick sale for cash, desire to realize a percentage over cost, or desire to realize maximum yield no matter how low the cost.

(3) Region. U.S., Canada, Asia, Europe, other?

(4) Cash or trade. Part of a large volume deal involving a "lot" of reels.

(5) Who is the buyer? Hobby collector, or a dealer needing to buy at a price low enough to allow for mark-up.

Another point to consider is that some of the scarce reels described herein have sold at specialized tackle auctions at a range of prices substantially higher than our analysis would indicate was typical. Clearly, astounding prices can and have been realized at auction. Should you ever have a particularly rare and apparently valuable reel to sell — a specialized fishing tackle auction may be a prudent marketing choice. In any case, this value guide is provided for the hobby collector and is not intended to be a complete investment analysis. Independent investigation of value and the services of an experienced appraiser are recommended, especially when engaging in speculation for profit.

ABBEY & IMBRIE

	poor-fair	good-vg	excellent
Takapart multiplier by Meisselbach (c.1910)	$12	$30	$55
"St. Lawrence" nickel plated casting reel (c.1917)	10	20	40
Perfection brass/nickel trout reel by Hendryx	12	30	55
Brass trout reel w/ ring-clamp (hooks trademark) 1895	40	110	225
Brass trout reel (hooks TM) pull-up stop latch c.1895	35	100	200
Andrew Clerk . N.Y. pre-A&I brass trout reel (c.1860)	150	300	500
New York style ball-handle bay reel c.1875	100	200	350
"Sea Bright" nickel & bakelite bay reel	7	18	40
Nickel multiplier by Julius Vom Hofe (1889 patent)	18	35	65
Nickel casting reel - rim control drag (JVH 1882 pat.)	55	125	235
Silver and hard rubber trout reel c.1890 by Conroy	200	350	650
Silver and hard rubber 3" trout reel (1892 patent)	90	170	330
Automatic fly reel with lineguide (c.1915)	15	40	80
"Salmo" fly reel #238,300 (c.1928) some w/ agate LG	12	28	45

ABU (Sweden)

	poor-fair	good-vg	excellent
Ambassadeur #1500C UL ball bearings c.1978	14	32	60
Ambassadeur #1750 UL narrow spool baitcaster	12	30	55
Ambassadeur #2000 (red sideplates) c. 1958	12	30	55
Ambassadeur #2050 (red sideplate with pearl insert)	14	32	60
Ambassadeur #2600 with push button free-spool	15	35	60
Ambassaseur #2650 narrow spool	16	38	70
Ambassadeur #2500C (1970's)	14	32	60
Ambassadeur #3000,4000	14	32	60
Ambassadeur #4500 red c.1975	14	30	55
Ambassadeur #4500C ball bearings - narrow spool	16	38	70
Ambassadeur #4600C narrow spool (c.1978)	16	38	70
Ambassadeur #5000 (c.1965) dual pearl crank knobs	15	35	65

Ambassadeur #5000A large capacity spool	14	30	55
Ambassadeur #5000B large capacity and CB handle	15	35	65
Ambassadeur #5000C black rims, ball bearings	12	30	50
Ambassadeur #5000D green (c.1970's)	10	26	45
Ambassadeur #5500C ball bearings c.1975	12	30	55
Ambassadeur #5600C (fast cast thumber)	12	35	60
Ambassadeur #6000 wide spool	12	30	55
Ambassadeur #6000C	14	35	60
Ambassadeur #6500C	14	35	60
Ambassadeur #7000C	14	35	60
Ambassadeur #6600C (c.1979 with fast cast)	14	35	60
Ambassadeur #5000 De Luxe (gold) in wood box	110	300	550
Ambassadeur #9000C,10000CA ocean, auto low-gear	22	55	95
Record casting reels 1940 -1950's (#1300,1600)	15	35	70
Record "Sport" #2100 (narrow spool)	20	45	90
Abu 444 spinning reel c.1955	8	16	35
Abu (Zebco) Cardinal spinning reel #3 ultra light	15	38	70
Abu (Zebco) Cardinal #4	10	26	65
Abu-matic closed faced reel c.1960 #120 -160	3	9	17
Abu-matic #170 (star drag)	3	12	20
Abu #505-520 no bail spinning reel	3	12	20
Abu-Delta triangular fly reel (#3-5)	6	20	38

AIREX

	poor-fair	good-vg	excellent
Bache Brown Mastereel circa 1950	3	13	25
Spinster spinning reel	2	8	15
Larchmont spinning reel	3	10	20
Vic spinning reel	2	6	12
Beachcomber saltwater spinning reel	3	9	18

ALCEDO (Italy)

	poor-fair	good-vg	excellent
Micron ultra-light spinning reel	15	40	80
#2 - cs medium fresh water spinning reel	10	30	50
Mark 4 and Mark 5 deluxe salt water spinning reels	15	35	75

ALLCOCK (England)

	poor-fair	good-vg	excellent
Stanley - spinning reel c. 1925	25	70	160
Felton Crosswind - spinning reel	15	30	60
Conquest - single action fly reel (stag trademark)	18	45	85
3" trout reel (black) with red agate lineguide c.1930	20	50	95
Bronzed brass trout fly reel (oval trademark) c.1890	30	65	100
Marvel - 3" fly reel with lineguide	20	50	90
"Popular" - narrow spool fly reel	15	30	50
"Black Knight" aluminum fly reel	15	30	50
Aerialite - bakelite ocean reel with lineguide	8	18	35
Aerial reel - aluminum alloy case and drum c.1925	35	75	140
Easicast reel (Silex style with twin handles)	10	30	50

ALVEY (Australia)

	poor-fair	good-vg	excellent
Sidecast reel (surf) - red marbled plastic	4	12	22
Trolling models	4	9	18
Children's reel (c.1960)	4	10	20

ASHAWAY

	poor-fair	good-vg	excellent
"Slip Cast" spinning reel (aluminum) Ohio	5	18	35

BATE, T.H.

	poor-fair	good-vg	excellent
Pre-Civil War ball-handle brass reel (New York)	200	400	700

BILLINGHURST

	poor-fair	good-vg	excellent
1859 Patent - birdcage design antique reel	350	600	1100

BRISTOL

	poor-fair	good-vg	excellent
#65 single action fly reel c.1939	3	9	18
#66 single action fly reel c.1939	3	9	18
'Electromatic" level wind multiplying reel	6	20	40

STAN BOGDAN

	poor-fair	good-vg	excellent
Stan Bogdan No. 0 handmade salmon fly reel	400	800	1400
Stan Bogdan No. 00 handmade salmon fly reel	400	800	1400
Stan Bogdan steelhead fly reel	400	850	1500
"Baby Bogdan" trout size fly reel (wide spool)	450	900	1600
"Baby Bogdan" trout size fly reel	450	900	1600

BRONSON

	poor-fair	good-vg	excellent
Take-apart fly reel (some with agate lineguide)	8	22	45
Royalist #370 single action fly reel	3	9	15
Multi-Royal #380 fly reel (c.1965)	3	9	15
Royalmatic #390 automatic fly reel	2	4	9
Union Jack - skeleton fly reel (c.1960)	2	5	9
Black Hawk - medium spinning reel	3	8	14
Sea Wolf #290 - saltwater spinning reel (c.1965)	3	10	18
Buddy #800 - ultralight spinning reel (c.1960)	2	5	9
Regent #990 - spin cast reel in vinyl case	2	5	10
Wildcat #804 - spin cast reel	2	4	6
#880 - saltwater spin cast reel (c.1965)	3	5	8
Meteor #1500 level wind direct drive baitcasting reel	2	4	9
Victor #1000 level wind baitcasting reel (c.1960)	2	4	6
Falcon #170 level wind trolling reel	3	6	10

Fleetwing #2475 level wind all-metal baitcaster	3	6	10
Fleetwing all metal baitcaster (early model c. 1940)	5	10	20
Lashless #1700 levelwind (c.1955)	3	5	9
Sport King #81 nickel baitcaster	3	6	10
Veteran #1010 levelwind baitcaster (c.1960)	3	6	10
Veteran #1100 with anti-backlash (early c.1932)	5	10	20
Biltwell #3300 jeweled multiplier (twin wood knobs)	6	17	28
Flyer #2450 level wind baitcaster	3	6	10
"Modern" level wind baitcaster (early c. 1930)	6	15	25
"The Blue Heron" #3800 (nickel silver) c.1930	7	18	35
#3600 jeweled - baitcaster c.1931	5	10	20
#3700 jeweled - baitcaster	5	10	20
"Go-Getter" bronzed brass baitcaster (early Bronson)	6	12	25
"J.A. Coxe" model 26 Invader (star drag) baitcaster	4	10	20
"J.A. Coxe" model 25c Coronet (light free-spool c.1965)	9	28	55
"Bronson Coronet 25N" free-spool	10	30	65
"J.A. Coxe" model 190 star drag salt water reel	6	15	25

CARLTON

	poor-fair	good-vg	excellent
Skeleton design 2 1/2" nickel trout reel	18	30	50
Automatic fly reel c.1915 Rochester N.Y.	20	45	90
"Bait Caster" 1903 Patent (black plate inserts) thumber	110	195	350
Multiplier #9 (10/27/08 patent) click & brake switches	55	105	195
"Ideal" single action fly reel c.1900	20	35	60
"Lightweight" quick take-down frame fly reel c.1900	25	45	85

CEMM

	poor-fair	good-vg	excellent
Fly reel c.1950 Vancouver B.C. Canada	25	55	115

CONROY

	poor-fair	good-vg	excellent
"J.C. Conroy & Co. N.Y." small brass ball handle	150	350	650
"Conroys Maker" c.1850 (pinned plate) large brass	200	450	800
"Thomas J. Conroy Maker N.Y." salmon reel (rubber)	125	275	550
"J. Conroy Maker" c.1860 brass with rosewood knob	150	325	650
"Thos. Conroy & J.V.Hofe" trout reel (hard rubber)	140	250	500
"Conroy, Bissett & Malleson" (post Cvil War) brass reels	150	325	650
Thomas J. Conroy #2 size - rubber & metal trout reel	175	350	700

J.A. COXE

	poor-fair	good-vg	excellent
4/0 size saltwater reel c.1930 (early)	60	150	300
6/0 size big game reel (early California made)	85	175	325
9/0 size big game reel c.1930 California made	125	250	400
12/0 size big game reel - later Bronson, Michigan	125	275	450
14/0 size big game reel	125	300	600
16/0 size "Zane Grey" model c.1935 big game reel	250	500	900
Model 325 star drag saltwater reel	6	15	35
Model 625 saltwater reel (Bronson, Mich.)	6	15	35
Model 630 saltwater bay reel	6	15	30
Model 850 saltwater reel	7	25	50
Model 10-2 baitcaster with spring loaded ivory knobs	8	20	40
Model 10-C multiplying baitcaster	6	15	30
Model 15-C multiplying baitcaster	6	15	30
Model 25	9	25	45
Model 25-2 dual ivory knobs, german silver	14	30	65
Model 25-3 level-wind multiplier	14	30	65
Model 25-C freespool (German Silver)	14	30	65
Model 25 (narrow spool) baitcaster	15	40	75
Model 60-C baitcaster	6	15	30

THOS. CHUBB

	poor-fair	good-vg	excellent
2" Heavy brass crank reel (Pflueger mfg.)	12	30	50
"Thos. H. Chubb" rubber-nickel (Vom Hofe mfg)	35	70	115
Raised pillar nickeled brass trout reel c.1905	15	40	65

COZZONE

	poor-fair	good-vg	excellent
Hard rubber and silver trout click reel c.1930	40	75	165
"German Silver" medium saltwater reel	35	70	135

DAIWA (Japan)

	poor-fair	good-vg	excellent
EXP-475 deluxe fly reel (only about 500 made)	100	200	300

DUNCAN-BRIGGS

	poor-fair	good-vg	excellent
Level wind multiplying reels c. 1950	3	8	15
Fly reels c. 1950	3	8	15

FARLOW (England)

	poor-fair	good-vg	excellent
C. Farlow & Co. early brass and hard rubber fly reels	95	175	300
Bronzed brass trout reel with horn knob c.1870	45	90	150
"Regal" ball bearing salmon fly reel c.1920	35	80	150
"Heyworth" silent check fly reel c.1935	30	60	90
"Grenaby" trout fly reel c.1935	20	45	85
"Grenaby" trout fly reel c. 1966	12	30	55
"Kennet" fly reel with agate lineguide c.1930	30	70	125
"BWP" fly reel c.1930	40	85	150
"Saphire" trout fly reel c.1960	15	35	60
"Cobra" wide spool salmon fly reel (3 1/2 inch)	15	40	75
"Python" fly reel - salmon size 4 inch c.1960	15	40	70
"Serpent" fly reel c.1965	15	35	60
"Ambassador" 4 inch salmon fly reel c.1966	15	35	60

"President" 3 1/2 inch fly reel c.1966 15 35 60

FIN-NOR

	poor-fair	good-vg	excellent
No. 1 trout or 2 steelhead-salmon fly reels c.1975	60	135	250
No. 2 salmon fly reel older "Wedding Cake" back	175	400	600
No. 3 Anti-Reverse salt water fly reel c. 1975	80	175	300
Fin-Nor big game trolling reels c.1940-1950's	135	275	450
Fin-Nor gold anodized deluxe spinning reels	75	180	295

FOLLET

	poor-fair	good-vg	excellent
Birdcage design Civil War era (horizontal style)	200	600	1100

FOX

	poor-fair	good-vg	excellent
Level wind multipliers (pear-hex shaped plates)	5	15	30
Bay reels (bakelite plates-similar to early Penn)	7	18	35

J.J. FROST

	poor-fair	good-vg	excellent
"Kelso" heavy automatic fly reel (1907 patent)	15	35	70

GAYLE

	poor-fair	good-vg	excellent
Handmade G.W. Gayle & Son baitcaster c.1890	350	875	1800
Handmade german silver Gayle saltwater reels	450	1100	2000
Handmade by Gayle - Wm. Mills "Intrinsic" baitcaster	300	700	1500
Gayle "Simplicity" side mount reel c. 1925	9	20	30
Gayle "Simplicity" #3 fly reel stamped metal c.1930	5	10	20
Gayle "Simplicity" #6 fly reel (dual knobs) c.1930	5	10	20
Gayle "Simplicity" #5 fly reel (perforated spool)	5	10	20

GOITE

	poor-fair	good-vg	excellent
Indiana style with lineguide and twin knobs	18	35	55

HARDY (England)

	poor-fair	good-vg	excellent
"Perfect" early 1896 check - brass face or all brass	175	400	700
"Perfect" 1896 check, wide spool large diameter	200	550	850
"Perfect" 1906 check 3 5/8", rotating line guide	125	300	500
"Perfect" 1912 check 3 7/8", ivorine handle, brass foot	95	250	395
"Perfect" c.1928 - 1955 MK. II check 2 7/8" - 3 1/8"	65	175	245
"Perfect" fly reel same with agate line guide	75	195	295
"Perfect" c. 1928 - 1955 MK. II check 3 3/8" and larger	55	150	210
"Perfect" fly reel same with agate line guide	60	160	235
"Perfect" wide spool salmon fly reel - MK. II check	80	190	325
"Special Perfect" c.1910 (3 1/4" with raised face)	300	700	1300
"Bougle" trout fly reel c. 1910 (hand & rod trademark)	400	1200	2400
"Hercules" bronzed fly reels c. 1897 (oval trademark)	100	250	400
"St. George" pre-1950 (3 screw spool release) 3" size	75	200	425
"St. George" later (2 screw spool release) 3" size	60	175	300
"St. George Jr." 2 9/16" diameter trout fly reel	100	275	500
"St. George pre-1950 (3 3/8 " and 3 3/4" size)	65	150	265
"St. George later c. 1965 (3 3/8" and 3 3/4" size)	50	125	200
"Uniqua" c. 1915 - 1930 (horseshoe style spool latch)	40	85	150
"Uniqua" c. 1930 - 1960 (telephone style spool latch)	35	75	140
"Uniqua" small sizes 2 5/8" or 2 7/8"	50	135	195
"Uniqua" heavy salmon size 4" with OIL style latch	45	90	175
"Sunbeam" trout fly reel, old MK. II check 2 3/4" size	40	85	165
"Sunbeam" c.1960 approx. 3" with brass line guide	30	60	120
"Sunbeam" c.1970 lightweight, with clip-in agate	35	65	130
"St. John" salmon fly reel 3 7/8" diameter c.1925	40	85	165
"St. John" modern version c.1970	30	60	135
"The Fly Reel" (c.1947) (nickel-silver lineguide)	75	175	300
"Davy" fly reel with narrow perforated spool c.1930	350	750	1500

"Cascapedia" c.1935 ebonite Vom Hofe style fly reel	900	3800	7000
"Lightweight" early aluminum solid spool c. 1937	45	95	180
"Princess" first model with green finish	40	90	175
"Flyweight" (early pre-1965 with 2 screw lineguard)	25	65	105
"Flyweight" (same with silent drag)	30	75	115
"Featherweight" (2 screw heavy silver line guide)	25	65	105
"LRH Lightweight" (2 screw line guide)	25	65	105
"Princess" (2 screw line guide)	30	75	125
"St. Aidan" large diameter (3 3/4") lightweight reel	35	85	135
"Gem" and "Hydra" fly reels	15	35	60
"Viscount" fly reels (i.e #140,150)	15	40	70
"Zenith" and "Husky" salmon fly reels (wide spool)	40	100	175
"Fortuna" fly reels (silent brake) anti-reverse c.1927	200	600	900
"The Silex" c.1900 (some with jeweled bearing)	75	150	300
"Silex #2 (c.1915) twin ivory knobs	60	125	235
"Silex Major" c.1925	60	125	235
"Super Silex" c.1930	90	200	350
"Elarex" level wind baitcaster with thumb rest c.1955	40	80	135
"Jock Scott" deluxe multiplier c.1952	100	225	400
"Altex" spinning reel (first model made in 1932)	35	75	140
"Altex" fixed spool spinning reels c.1935- 1950's	25	65	115
"Hardex" c.1938 half-bail spinning reel	15	40	65
"Exalta" spinning reel c. 1960	20	55	90

HEDDON

	poor-fair	good-vg	excellent
Dowagiac (similar to Meisselbach "Tri-Part")	25	50	75
No. 30 multiplier (W. Carter design - Horton parts)	75	175	300
No. 35 (similar to Bluegrass #3) c. 1918	75	175	300
No. 40 (similar to Horton Bluegrass #25) c.1918	55	100	200
No. 45 (similar to Simplex #33) c. 1918	50	95	175

	poor-fair	good-vg	excellent
"3-15" (number 3 size, original cost $15) c. 1920 -27	65	165	225
"3-24" multiplier c. 1920	65	165	225
"3-30" some with clear sapphire jeweled bearings	65	175	295
"4-15" multiplier (unusual wand style levelwind)	100	325	650
"4-18" similar to above c. 1923 (unique design)	100	300	600
"3-35" multiplier c. 1925	60	160	275
"3-25" multiplier c.1930	50	120	200
"Lone Eagle" #206 - level wind multiplier	20	40	60
"Chief Dowagiac" #4 - level wind multiplier c.1932	25	50	75
"White House Angler" - #215 level wind (c.1930)	30	60	90
"Pal" Model #P41 c.1950	8	20	35
"Pal" Model #P41N	9	22	40
"Heritage" Mark III disengaging LW free spool c.1965	9	25	45
"Imperial" #125 single action fly reels	15	38	65
#320 fly reel "Daisy" (green) some made in Japan	4	15	25
"Mark IV" automatic fly reels c. 1960	2	4	9
"Automatic - Free Stripping" fly reel J.H. Sons c. 1940	6	14	25
"Spin Pal" spinning reel c. 1950	5	12	20
"Spin Pal" #100 and #200 spin cast reels c. 1967	2	5	10
"Winona" c. 1930 - 1950 unaltered with lineguide intact	9	25	45
"Winona" c.1920 pre-Heddon (Boyer)	10	30	50

A. HENDRYX

	poor-fair	good-vg	excellent
Raised pillar brass trout reels (2-2 1/2")	6	14	22
Nickel plated brass trout reels c.1900	6	14	22
Simple casting reels	8	20	35
Ornate "S" handle or patented oil cap features	10	25	45
"Revonoc" brand and similar small multipliers	7	18	30
Saltwater bay reel (#5009)	10	22	45

HERMOS

	poor-fair	good-vg	excellent
Ferris-wheel style trolling reels	10	20	40

H & I

	poor-fair	good-vg	excellent
Plastic "Vernley" single action fly reel	2	5	10
Horrocks-Ibbotson "Admiral" baitcaster (c.1938)	4	9	15
Horrocks-Ibbotson bait casting and spinning reels	4	8	12
"Dolphin" salt water reel	5	9	15
"Seaking" salt water reel	5	9	15
Horrocks-Ibbotson "Utica" automatic fly reel	2	5	9
Horrocks-Ibbotson "Y&E" auto. c.1925 - 1935	15	30	50

HORTON MFG. CO.

	poor-fair	good-vg	excellent
"Meek" No. 2 german silver multiplier (Conn.)	140	285	425
"Meek" No. 3 german silver multiplier (Conn.)	95	185	310
"Bluegrass" No. 3 (Bristol, Conn.)	80	170	280
"Bluegrass" No. 4 (Bristol Conn.)	80	170	280
"Simplex" No. 25 (Bristol, Conn.)	60	120	200
Horton "Meek" No. 30 level wind baitcaster	50	110	190
"Bluegrass Simplex" Free Spool No. 34	40	85	165
"Bluegrass Simplex" No. 33	40	80	155
"Bluegrass" #10 levelwind (hinged carriage) c.1930	25	55	110
"Meek" #55, #56 fly reels (similar to Hardy Uniqua)	30	65	125

HUMPHREYS

	poor-fair	good-vg	excellent
Denver, Colorado stainless steel spin type	10	20	38

ILLINGWORTH

	poor-fair	good-vg	excellent
#1 early British spinning type reel c.1906	200	400	600
#2 (2nd model) c. 1910	40	80	150

	poor-fair	good-vg	excellent
#3 (c. 1920)	35	70	130
Fixed spool style spinning reel (later models)	20	40	70

KEEN CASTER

	poor-fair	good-vg	excellent
Ravena Metal Works (Seattle, Washington)	3	5	10
(Early) Bellingham, Washington (pat.pending)	6	18	35
Later Bellingham, Washington	4	6	12

HENRY KIEST

	poor-fair	good-vg	excellent
Indiana (ferris wheel) style reel sold c.1930 in tin can	10	25	45

KALAMAZOO

	poor-fair	good-vg	excellent
"Atlas" level wind casting reel #1708 (c.1950)	4	8	17
"Pride" level wind casting reel	4	8	17
Skeleton style fly reel similar to "Progress"	5	9	1
Model 23 (thumbless baitcasting reel) unusual housing	10	20	40
"Utility" reel #1700 (packaged in tin can) value in original can	12	28	50

H.H. KIFFE

	poor-fair	good-vg	excellent
Quality salt water trolling reels (c. 1885)	30	65	110
Later salt water bay reels	15	30	50
Bait casting reels c.1900	20	40	80

KOVALOVSKY

	poor-fair	good-vg	excellent
Custom Big Game Reels 1935 and later	400	1100	2300

LANGLEY

	poor-fair	good-vg	excellent
"Speedcast" level wind baitcaster c.1950	4	7	14
"Reelcast" level wind baitcaster c. 1950	4	7	14
"Castrite" baitcasting multiplier	5	8	15

	poor-fair	good-vg	excellent
"Streamlite" level wind multiplier c. 1950	5	10	20
"Lurecast" LW multiplier	5	10	20
"Plugcast" LW multiplier	5	10	20
Target model #340 deluxe baitcaster c. 1950	9	20	40
Langley aluminum single action fly reels	5	9	17
"Spinlite" spin reel	4	7	14
"Spinflow" model spin reel (c.1956)	3	6	11

LEONARD - MILLS

	poor-fair	good-vg	excellent
Philbrook & Paine (pre-1877 Leonard patent)	2000	4500	9000
H.L. Leonard 1st model fly reel (marbled face)	1500	3500	8000
H.L. Leonard 1877 patent "Bi-Metal" trout reel	600	1300	2500
H. L. Leonard pat.#191813 (hard rubber) fly reel	225	450	700
Leonard-Mills trout reels (german silver & rubber)	190	300	600
William Mills & Son (Leonard trout and salmon reels)	190	300	600
William Mills & Son N.Y. "Fairy" 2 inch trout reel	300	600	1100
William Mills "Dry Fly" light salmon reel	195	325	625
Leonard-Mills Model 33 Midge reel (c.1925)	200	385	650
Leonard Model 50 trout reel	195	375	625
"Leonard" fly reels c. 1984	100	250	400
Wm. Mills & Son (Leonard) Gear Reel w/1882 pat.	2500	5000	9500
William Mills c.1940 salmon fly reels similar to Hardy	60	110	175

LUXOR (France)

	poor-fair	good-vg	excellent
Pezon & Michel (anodized green finish) No.1-S	8	27	55
Luxor No.1-S "Manual" (circa 1957) no bail	7	20	40
Luxor No.1 (1-S but gray, non-folding handle)	7	22	45
Luxor No.2-R medium spinning reel (circa 1957)	7	22	45
Luxor No. 2-RG manual version (no bail)	7	20	40
Luxor No. 3 Heavy salt water spinning reel	7	22	45

MAGIC REEL CO.

	poor-fair	good-vg	excellent
Spin reel (Denver) c. 1950 with side-arm	15	30	55

MALLOCH(Scotland)

	poor-fair	good-vg	excellent
Sidecaster - Scotland (spinning reel) c. 1885	70	135	200
Sidecaster small 3 inch size c. 1890	75	150	215
Bronzed brass salmon fly reels c.1925	45	85	175
Sun & Planet style fly reels	70	145	235

ALEX MARTIN

	poor-fair	good-vg	excellent
The "Thistle" 3 inch trout fly reels (Scotland)	40	95	165
"Thistle" ball bearing salmon size reels	35	85	150
The "Caledonia" lightweight fly reel	30	70	125

MARTIN REEL CO.

	poor-fair	good-vg	excellent
Early automatic fly reels (c.1925) #1 - #5	5	10	20
Automatic fly reel "flywate" #27,#28 c.1930	3	6	10
"Flywate" fly reel later c.1950 - 1960	2	5	8
"Tuffy" model #81 upright automatic	2	4	7
"Tuffy" model #96 horizontal automatic c. 1965	2	4	7
"Blue Chip" automatic fly reel (#83,73) c.1963	2	5	9
Model #7 single action fly reel (dual knobs) c.1960	2	4	8
Model #43 single action trout reel "Reel-Tuff"	2	4	8

MEEK

	poor-fair	good-vg	excellent
J.F. Meek Frankfort, Ky. multiplier c.1840	1500	3000	5000
J.F. and B.F. Meek Ky, multiplier c.1850	900	2000	4000
Meek and Milam, Ky. multipliers c.1865	800	1700	3000
B.F. Meek Louisville, multipliers c.1882	225	450	700

	poor-fair	good-vg	excellent
B.F. Meek and Sons, Louisville #2 c.1890	165	300	500
B.F. Meek and Sons #3 multiplier c. 1890	120	200	385
B.F. Meek and Sons #3 "Bluegrass" c.1895	110	185	325
B.F. Meek and Sons #4 c.1890 - 1895	120	200	375
B.F. Meek and Sons #25 (Carter's Patent) c.1907	70	135	210
B.F. Meek and Sons #33 (Carter's Patent) c.1907	50	90	160
B.F. Meek #44 fly reel	2000	6000	10000

B.C. MILAM

	poor-fair	good-vg	excellent
B.C. Milam - Frankfort, Kentucky #2-4 multipliers	275	600	1000
B.C. Milam and Son c.1890 multipliers	200	400	700
B.C. Milam and Son c.1910 - 1925 (i.e. "Rustic")	100	200	300

MEISSELBACH

	poor-fair	good-vg	excellent
"Takapart" #480 series multiplier (c. 1910)	8	25	40
"Tripart" #580 series multiplier	8	25	40
"Tripart" or "Takapart" freespool	10	30	50
Simmons Special "Tripart" private label	9	28	45
Kingfisher brand "Tripart" or Takapart	9	28	45
"Okey" multiplier #625	18	40	75
Symploreel multiplier #255	25	55	100
Symploreel multiplier #752 (c.1927)	15	35	65
"Flyer" level-wind multiplier (c.1928)	8	25	40
No. 100 Bull's-eye levelwind multiplier (c.1929)	9	22	38
No. 110 Bull's-eye with bakelite spool (c.1930)	9	22	38
#250 Featherlight single action fly reel (1904 pat.)	10	30	55
#260 Featherlight fly reel	10	30	55
#270 Featherlight single action fly reel (1896 pat.)	12	35	60
"Expert" single action fly reel #9 (c. 1886)	15	40	75
"Expert" fly reel #11 early	15	40	75

	poor-fair	good-vg	excellent
"Expert" fly reel #13 early	15	40	75
"Expert" fly reel #19 (1889 patent date) later	12	35	65
"Rainbow" single action fly reel #627, #631	5	15	28
"Rainbow" fly reel (with early telephone latch) c.1916	9	28	60
#370, 372 fly reel (some with line guide)	10	30	65
"Symploreel" fly reel (c.1929)	12	35	70
Automatic fly reel (patented 1914) German silver	20	50	90
Automatic fly reel #665 (c. 1920)	10	35	75
Automatic #660 Autofly	10	30	65
"Neptune" saltwater trolling reels c.1920	12	25	50
"Neptune" later model (ext. handle c. 1935)	10	20	40
"Sea-Line" #75,85 bay reels c.1932	6	18	35
Meisselbach "Good Luck" wood reel (1897 pat.)	20	45	90
Meisselbach "Good Luck" wood reel with drag	25	50	95

MITCHELL (France)

	poor-fair	good-vg	excellent
Early C.A.P. (Carpano & Pons) spinning reels	12	25	50
"Spinnette" c.1955 spinning reel	3	6	10
Garcia #304 spinning reel c.1965	3	6	12
Garcia #300 spinning reel (301 left-hand model)	3	9	20
#300 DL (Deluxe presentation box, gold plating)	35	65	125
#410 (fast retrieve version of 300)	3	10	22
#308 ultra-light spinning reel	4	12	28
#408 (fast retrieve version of 308)	4	15	30
#306 medium spinning reel	3	9	20
#406 (fast retrieve version of 306)	3	10	22
#302 large capacity saltwater spinning reel	3	10	22
#402 fast retrieve with oversize knob (c.1970)	4	12	24
#386,486 corrosion resistant saltwater reels	4	12	24
#488 big game drag, spinning reel	9	28	55

	poor-fair	good-vg	excellent
Garcia-Mitchell #622 star drag multiplying reel	5	15	30
Garcia-Mitchell #600A star drag casting reel	4	12	22
Garcia-Mitchell #1040,1060 (4/0 and 6/0) big game	40	80	150
Garcia-Mitchell #710 automatic fly reel	3	6	9
Garciamatic No.1430 auto fly reel (c.1960)	3	6	9

MONTAGUE

	poor-fair	good-vg	excellent
"Yankee" saltwater bay multiplying reel	4	10	22
"Gulf" saltwater reel	4	10	22
"Atlantic" surf or bay reel	5	12	25
"Fishkill" saltwater reel	5	12	25
"Clipper" saltwater	5	12	25
"Pacific" trolling salwater reel	8	18	35
"Longbeach" surf or trolling reel	8	18	35
"Offshore" trolling reel	12	25	45
"Imperial" big game reels (german silver)	45	95	155
"Tarpon" early 500 yd. capacity reel	30	50	100
"Waterwitch" bakelite single action reel	8	15	35
"Bakelite and nickel" trout reels c.1930	9	18	38
"Professional" baitcasting reel (non-level wind)	4	10	22

OCEAN CITY

	poor-fair	good-vg	excellent
#35,36 single action fly reel	3	6	12
#76,77 single action fly reels	3	7	14
"X-pert" single action fly reel	4	9	20
"Wanita" single action fly reel (c.1935)	3	6	12
#90 automatic fly reel (manual knobs)	4	8	15
"Fortesque" (nickel silver) saltwater trolling reel	15	25	55
"Sea Girt" saltwater reel (c. 1930)	10	20	40
"IKE Walton" trolling reel	20	40	70

	poor-fair	good-vg	excellent
"Long Key" 450,500 & 600 yd. size big game reel	18	38	65
"Panama" (10/0 - 14/0) big game reels c.1935	50	110	200
"Balboa" 10/0 big game reel	40	100	175
"Bay City" saltwater multiplier (c.1940)	4	10	20
"Inductor" saltwater bay reel (c.1950)	5	12	22
"Brigantine" saltwater bay reel (c.1939)	5	12	25
"Chelsea" saltwater bay reel (c.1930)	5	14	30
"Fantum" alloy saltwater multiplier (c.1938)	5	12	25
Ocean City bay reels (c.1960-1970)	3	6	14
#50 baitcasting reel (sold by L.L. Bean) c.1954	4	10	20
"Trojan" black alloy tournament reel (c.1937)	6	15	35
#970 level wind multiplier c.1950	5	10	20
#300 spinning reel	3	7	18
#350 spinning reel	4	8	20

ORVIS

	poor-fair	good-vg	excellent
1874 patented fly reel (in original walnut box)	N/A	1000	2000
1874 fly reel (riveted construction) no wood box	200	400	800
CFO fly reels (modern machined, made in England)	20	40	85
Model 50 spinning reel (made in Italy) c.1965	7	20	40
Model 75A spinning reel	6	15	35
Model 100 spinning reel (designed by Fiat)	6	15	35
Model 100SS and 150SS (c. 1975)	6	18	38
Orvis 300 spinning reel	6	14	30
Orvis 200 saltwater spinning reel c.1963	6	14	30

PENN

	poor-fair	good-vg	excellent
Atlantic No.14 wood knob (c.1948 and earlier)	3	7	18
Penn #15 early bay reel (c.1939) 300d knob	4	8	20
Penn No. 80 wood knob (200 yd.) c.1939 later	4	8	20

Penn No. 249 double multiplier (early wood knob)	4	8	20
Penn No. 149 bottom fishing - free spool reel	4	8	20
Penn No. 49 multiplier c.1950 or newer	4	9	22
Super Mariner No. 49M (c.1970)	6	12	25
Penn No. 85 star drag / free spool c.1950 - 1970	3	6	10
Delmar No. 285 star drag bay reel c. 1950 - 1970	3	6	11
Long Beach No. 60 thru 68 trolling reels c.1950 - 1970	4	8	20
Penn No. 190 (c.1948) wood knob 100 yd. size	3	7	18
Penn No. 180 (star darg), 185 free spool 100 yd.	3	7	18
Penn No. 155,160 casting and surf reels	3	7	18
Surfmaster No. 150,200,250 c. 1940's - 1970	5	12	25
Squidder No. 140, 145 (BB - air brake spool)	6	18	30
Squidder No. 146 narrow plastic spool c. 1970's	6	20	35
Sea Scamp, Sea Hawk (No. 78, 77) economy reels	3	5	8
Silver Beach No. 99	4	9	18
Jigmaster No. 500 (c.1960) classic red model	5	14	28
Jigmaster No. 501 (c.1960) narrow spool	5	15	30
Penn No. 109 earlier model c. 1940's	4	12	22
Penn Peer levelwind (i.e 9,109,209) c.1970 to date	4	12	22
Penn 309 large capacity level wind	5	14	28
Senator (older models with wood knob) c.1938	10	20	45
Senators 1/0 - 3/0 deep sea reels	9	20	40
Senators 4/0 - 6/0 big game	10	22	50
Senators 9/0 - 10/0 big game	20	40	80
Senators 12/0 - 16/0 big game	30	60	120
International gold big game reels (smaller #20,30)	35	75	165
International gold big game reels (large #80,130))	75	175	300
Levelmatifc 900 series (gold) baitcasters c. 1970	4	10	25
Spin fisher 700 series spinning reels c. 1970	4	9	22
Spinfisher 716 ultra-light spinning reel	4	10	25

PENNEL

	poor-fair	good-vg	excellent
"Tournament" jeweled casting reel (c.1919)	6	18	35
"Eagle" non-level wind 80 yd. (Montague Mfg)	6	15	30
"Silver Lake" 100 yd. dual-knobs	6	15	30
"Indian" non-level wind c.1925 (Montague Mfg)	6	15	30
"Special" NLW (c.1920) single ivoride knob	6	15	30

PFLUEGER

	poor-fair	good-vg	excellent
Supreme (first model, early) baitcaster	25	50	100
Supreme #1573 (c.1940)	6	18	38
Supreme #1575,76,77 (c.1965)	5	15	32
Supreme #510,511,513 star drag (c.1970)	5	15	32
Supreme #512 (knuckle buster)	5	14	28
Fastcast #1510	4	12	20
Summit #1993 baitcaster (c.1930's and later)	5	14	28
Nobby # 1963 baitcaster	4	12	20
Skillcast # 1953 baicaster (c.1940 - later)	4	12	20
Akron #1893 (60yd) and 1894 (80yd) early c.1930	5	15	30
Akron later models	4	10	18
#1944 multiplier (golden brass finish)c.1970	6	18	35
Procast # 1922, 2022 c.1940 tourny and skish caster	8	20	50
Trump #1943 baitcaster	4	8	15
Pard #1933 baitcaster (c.1940)	4	8	15
Four Brothers Trusty #1793 baitcaster (c.1940)	4	10	20
Four Brothers Regal (non-level wind) c.1920	5	14	25
Four Brothers Castwell #1323	5	15	28
Portage Pastime #1743 c.1940	4	10	20
Worth (c.1915)	10	30	60
Buckeye (1907 and 23 patent) early baitcaster	18	45	90

Four Brothers Sentrie casting reel	5	12	22
Atlas-Portage (early raised pillar trout reel)	6	12	25
Portage Niftee #1314	6	14	30
Portage Topic # 123 casting reel (early)	6	14	30
Portage "Seminole" (raised pillar, gun metal finish)	10	20	40
Redifor (c.1915) baitcaster	60	125	250
Rocket #1355 (star drag) 1345 (leather drag)	6	15	30
Norka #1335 saltwater trolling reel c.1940	6	15	32
Alpine (early c.1930) Williams drag	10	30	60
Alpine 2600 series c.1940	7	18	40
Atlapac No.1640 (4/0) saltwater game reel	20	40	80
Atlapac No.1660 (6/0) game reel c. 1940	30	65	135
Atlapac No.1690 (9/0) big game reel c.1938	40	85	175
Atlapac (older models) wood knob, german silver	40	85	175
Adams (6/0 and larger) deep sea reels	45	100	200
Templar No 1400 series c.1935	8	20	45
Akerite No.2068 surf casting reel c.1939	5	12	25
Capitol No. 1985,88,and 89. saltwater caster	5	14	30
Sea-Vue surf casting reel No.2048	4	9	18
Ohio No.1975,78, and 79 saltwater free-spool	5	14	30
Temco No. 2075,2078 bay reel bakelite (c.1941)	5	10	20
Temco (older model) metal 1923,26,27 patents	6	17	36
Four Brothers "Sumco" #2258 (same as Temco)	6	17	36
Autopla No.2475,79 (auto-no slack feature) c.1930	15	35	70
Interocean No.1885 (c.1940)	6	14	25
Interocean (older model c. 1925)	9	20	45
Golden West #1878 (small bay reel not the fly reel)	7	18	38
Bond No 2955 light saltwater casting reel	6	15	30
Oceanic (1907 and 1923 patents) c.1925	9	20	50
Everlaster (with leather thumb drag) c.1910-1930	10	22	50

184

	poor-fair	good-vg	excellent
Pontiac (with 1921 patent wood thumb brake)	10	22	50
Four Brothers "Mohawk" (similar to Pontiac)	10	22	50
Avalon - saltwater game reel (early 1907 patent)	18	45	95
Four Brothers "Beacon" nickel plated bay reel	7	18	38
Medalist fly reel #1492-96 (c.1935) early round LG	8	22	45
Medalist #1392,1394 (c.1940) no lineguide	6	17	35
Medalist #1492-98 (c.1950-1970) made in U.S.A.	6	18	35
Gem click fly reel #2094 early crescent spool latch	6	18	35
Gem fly reel #2094 w/coin slot spool release	4	12	25
Progress brass fly reel w/bulldog trademark (c.1920)	4	12	25
Progress click fly reel #1774 (aluminum c.1950)	3	6	13
Sal-Trout #1554 (gun metal or bronzed finish) c.1930	6	18	40
Sal-Trout #1558 trolling reel (dual knobs) nickel plated	5	10	20
Early all brass Sal-Trout with dual wood knobs	6	12	25
Superex #775,778 auto fly reel (1907 patent)	10	25	50
Hawkeye single action fly reel c.1928	40	110	250
Golden West fly reel (ebonite) c.1929	40	125	285
#577,578 Supreme fly reel (anti-reverse)	18	50	90
Four Brothers Delight click trout reel	25	60	135
Four Brothers Egalite click trout reel #1905	20	45	85
Pakron trolling reel #3180 (c.1938) twin wood knobs	6	17	35
Pakron #3178 (later model w/ counterbalance knob)	5	15	30
Captain #4128 single action trolling reel (twin knobs)	4	10	20
Taxie #3128 (c.1936) also #3138 with adj. drag	4	10	20
"Pelican" fresh water spinning reel model #1020	5	16	32
"Sea Star" salt water spinning reel model #1050	5	16	32
"Freespeed" spinning reel (c.1955)	3	6	12

PRECISION-BILT

	poor-fair	good-vg	excellent
"Mosquito" fly reel with transparent gear housing	10	25	50

QUICK (Germany)

	poor-fair	good-vg	excellent
Early D.A.M. spinning reels (c.1950)	4	15	35
#110 "microlite" spinning reel (c.1960)	4	15	35
#265 "microlite"	4	15	35
#110 N (c.1975)	4	12	28
#220,220 N	4	10	25
#330,330 N,331 N	4	10	25
#440,440 N, 441 N, 550N	4	12	28
"Finessa" 280	4	14	28
"Finessa" 330	4	14	28
Quick 101,103	3	8	17
Junior 240	3	8	17
"Standard"	4	10	20
Champion series baitcasting reels #700,800	10	20	45
Automatic fly reel D.A.M. (early)	5	15	28

RECORD (Swiss)

	poor-fair	good-vg	excellent
Spinning reels (half-bail style) c.1949	6	18	36

REDIFOR REEL CO.

	poor-fair	good-vg	excellent
Beetzsel (freespool LW) German silver (c. 1916)	75	150	350

ROCHESTER

	poor-fair	good-vg	excellent
Ideal #1,#2 silver click trout reels (1910 pat.)	12	40	85
Automatic fly reel (c.1910) similar to Kelso	20	45	90

SEAMASTER

	poor-fair	good-vg	excellent
Handmade fly reels (older models with dual knobs)	200	600	1300
Mark 2 single action salmon, bonefish size	150	500	1000

	poor-fair	good-vg	excellent
Anti-reverse models	175	550	1100
Mark 3 (dual mode) large tarpon fly reel	250	750	1800

SHAKESPEARE

	poor-fair	good-vg	excellent
Acme #1904 baitcasting reel (c.1950)	3	6	12
Acme #1901 (c.1965) green anodized	3	5	10
Classic #1972 HD (c.1938) jeweled end caps	5	12	22
Classic #1972 HF (c.1935) jeweled	5	12	22
Criterion #1960 GE (c.1945) jeweled	4	8	15
Criterion #1960 HD (c.1938) jeweled	4	9	17
Criterion #1961	5	10	18
"Deuce" level-wind multiplier	3	6	12
Direct Drive #1924 FK (c.1950)	4	10	20
Direct Drive #1926 FK (c.1950) green	4	10	20
Direct Drive #1924 S (c.1965) star drag	4	10	20
Direct Drive #1950 (c.1964)	3	6	12
Direct Drive #1937 (c.1965) free spool - star drag	5	12	22
"Favorite" non-level wind casting reel (c.1929)	5	12	22
Ideal #1963 (c.1930) baitcasting reel	4	9	20
"Intrinsic" (c.1910) Wm. Shakespeare Jr.	10	28	55
"Leader" early non-level wind casting reel	5	10	20
Marhoff #1964 GE (c.1946)	5	12	22
Marhoff #1964 HF (c.1935) marbled / unique	7	15	40
Marhoff (early c.1920) with patent markings	9	25	50
Precision #23041 early non-level wind (c.1918)	10	25	50
Precision #22641 (c.1912) counter balance handle	10	28	55
President #1970 A (c.1955-1965) pear side plates	6	14	28
Presidential Sportcast #1971 black & gold (c.1965)	7	15	30
Professional #1965 small LW casting reel (c.1950)	7	20	40
Standard Professional (c.1920) non-levelwind	12	35	65

Service #1944 GE (c.1946) large level-wind reel	5	10	20
Service #1944 FE (c.1956)	5	10	20
Service #1946 FA (c.1950)	5	10	20
Service #13042 non-LW (c.1910) Wm. Shakes. Jr.	12	38	70
Sportcast #1973 GE (c.1946) narrow spool level wind	9	18	35
Std. Sportcast #1977 GD (c.1947) narrow - jeweled	10	28	50
Sportcast #1982 (c.1965) push button freespool	5	12	22
Superior #1962 (c.1925) jeweled end caps	5	12	22
Super Sport #1969 (c.1970)	5	10	20
"Style B & C" Double shaft level-wind (c.1900) very early	85	175	325
Tournament #1744 HE (c.1936) narrow spool & free spool	18	40	75
True Blue #1956 GA (c.1940) basic nickel plated level-wind	3	6	12
True Blue #1956 GE (c.1946)	3	6	12
Triumph (early level wind c.1930)	5	10	20
Thrifty #1902 FG (c.1954) Nickel plated level wind	3	6	11
"Uncle Sam" early non-levelwind (c.1925)	10	25	50
"Universal Precision" early non-levelwind (c.1920)	9	22	45
Universal #2 (c.1905) 40yd marked "Quad" Wm. Shakes. Jr.	15	40	75
Universal #23038 (c.1910) larger capacity Wm. Shakes. Jr.	15	40	75
Wondereel #1920 GA (c.1940)	3	6	14
Wondereel #1920 FK (c.1951)	3	5	12
Deluxe Wondereel #1922 HB (c.1939)	4	8	18
Deluxe Wondereel #1922 FK (c.1951)	4	8	18
Light Wondereel #1921 FK (c.1951)	4	8	18
Wonder Troll Big Game Reels (c.1960)	20	65	125
Champion (Levelwind) ocean mooching reel	5	12	20
#1960 surfcasting reel	5	12	20
Bald Eagle #2205 salt water bay reel	6	17	35
Ocean Prince #2222,2223 trolling reel	8	18	38
Atlantis #2224 model33 bay reel	5	12	28

Jupiter (nickel silver bay reel)	15	38	75
Miller-Autocrat big game reels with case (c.1930)	60	135	250
Russel (single action fly reels) i.e. #1895 "intrinsic"	4	10	25
Sturdy fly reel #1861	3	8	20
Ausable fly reel (c.1950)	5	12	30
Model EC anti-reverse drag large fly reel (c.1970)	15	35	80
Automatic fly reel #1827,1836,1847 (The Tru-art)	3	8	18
Automatic fly reel #1821,1822,1824 (The OK)	3	6	12
"Kazoo" single action click fly reel (early c.1920)	6	18	38
"Winner" early click trout reel (black finish)	8	20	40
Wondercast #1775 FD (c.1957) spin casting reel	2	6	9
Wonderflyte #1776 (c.1965) spin cast reel	2	4	7

OGDEN SMITH (England)

	poor-fair	good-vg	excellent
"Zefer" trout fly reels (c.1930) some with ball-bearings	20	60	125
"Whitchurch" trout fly reel (some with silver drag on face)	18	45	90
Salmon fly reels (c.1935)	20	75	150

SOUTH BEND

	poor-fair	good-vg	excellent
#35,300,350 levelwind baitcasting reels (c.1950)	3	5	11
#400,450 casting reel	3	5	11
#55,550 casting reel (some older models w/antibacklash)	3	7	12
#650 casting reel (lightweight model)	3	6	12
#750 casting reel	3	6	12
#1000A, 1000C (early baitcasting reels)	7	14	28
#1131, 1200 (c.1915) high quality silver casting reels	10	25	50
#1250A (c.1935 high grade multiplier)	9	20	40
#1300 "Super South Bend" (c.1931) nickel silver multiplier	12	30	60
#2500 stainless steel baitcaster (c.1938) set in plastic case	35	85	175
#825,850 surf casting reel	4	9	16

#1110 Oreno Lite single action fly reel (c.1960)	2	3	5
#1110 Oreno fly reel (older model c.1932)	5	12	20
"Oreno" fly reel (c.1940) with lineguide	4	8	14
#1120 single action fly reel	2	4	6
#1150 marbled bakelite fly reel (c.1935)	2	5	8
"Finalist" single action fly reel	3	6	10
St. Joe click trout reel (c.1920) blued brass	10	25	40
#1130,1140,1150 Oreno Matic Automatic fly reels	2	4	8
Norseman #110 spin cast reel (c.1960)	2	5	8
#65-A spin cast reel (star drag)	2	3	5
#303 Futura deluxe model spin cast - spinning combo reel	2	4	6

WM. H. TALBOT

	poor-fair	good-vg	excellent
Early #2,3,4,5 sizes (c.1895) first model multipliers	150	350	750
Early Premier or Special models (dual handles, fancies etc)	175	400	800
Model #21,23,25,31,33,35,41,43,45 (c.1903 -1910)	135	250	650
Model 50 series high grade (saphire jeweled)	185	450	900
"Niangua" (c.1905) baitcaster	135	250	500
"Comet" (c.1910) baitcaster	110	225	450
"Mars" baitcaster	110	225	450
"Eli" Nevada, MO. baitcaster	110	225	450
"Star" model multiplier (c.1915 and later) K.C. MO.	95	195	325
Ben Hur fly reel (All German Silver more $ than aluminum)	500	2000	4000

THOMPSON REEL

	poor-fair	good-vg	excellent
Single action fly reels (F.T. Lovens - San Jose, Calif.)	95	225	450

UNION HARDWARE

	poor-fair	good-vg	excellent
"Sunnybrook" basic casting reel with painted knob	3	6	12
Black bakelite casting reel with emerald color jewels	9	20	40

	fair-good	good-vg	excellent
Inexpensive trout fly reels (c.1930)	2	5	9
Automatic fly reels	2	4	6

EDWARD VOM HOFE

	fair-good	good-vg	excellent
"Perfection" Model #360 trout fly reel (1896 patent)	400	1200	2600
"Peerless" Model #355 trout fly reel (1883 patent)	350	950	1700
"Tobique" Model #504 salmon fly reel (1896 patent)	250	500	1000
"Restigouche" Model #423 (1902,1883 or 1879 Pat.)	200	400	800
#560 surf casting reel	75	150	275
#521,621 (3/0-4/0) 1902 patent salt water reels	75	135	250
#621 (6/0) big game reel	95	165	300
#621 (9/0) big game reel	120	235	375
#721, 722 (10/0 - 14/0) "Commander Ross"	165	350	800
Antique Edward Vom Hofe (Silver) 1867 patent date	300	600	1200
#295 bass casting reel (1896 patent)	100	200	350

JULIUS VOM HOFE

	fair-good	good-vg	excellent
All metal trout reels1889 patent (star washer on back)	100	200	400
German silver and hard rubber trout reels (c.1890)	90	180	350
Baitcasting reels (hard rubber & nickel) 85,89 patent	30	55	100
Baitcasting reels with silver rims	40	70	135
Antique brass bay reel w/clover trade mark (c.1865)	250	400	700
B-Ocean big game reels (1911 patent) 2/0, 3/0	75	140	225
B-Ocean size 4/0	85	165	250
B-Ocean size 6/0	90	175	275
B-Ocean size 9/0	95	185	350
Nickel plated brass bay reel (1889 patent)	30	60	95
Frederich Vom Hofe & Son (Julius) c.1860 antique (silver)	300	600	1200

ARTHUR WALKER

	poor-fair	good-vg	excellent
TR-1 midge fly reel	225	450	900
TR-2 small trout fly reel	175	350	700
TR-3 trout fly reel	150	300	600

WEBER FLY CO.

	poor-fair	good-vg	excellent
"Henshall" brown bakelite fly reel (c.1930)	2	4	7

THOS. E. WILSON

	poor-fair	good-vg	excellent
Casting reels (i.e Model H545) 100 yd. circa 1910	15	25	40
Baitcasting reels with jeweled caps (c.1920)	18	30	50

WINCHESTER

	poor-fair	good-vg	excellent
Average saltwater reel (i.e.#2830) 300 yd. size	35	50	95
Small bay reels (i.e #2744) 100 yd. size	28	40	85
Raised pillar casting reels (i.e.#4142) c. 1920	35	55	100
Nickel plated raised pillar trout fly reels	40	75	110

WORDENS

	poor-fair	good-vg	excellent
Belt Reel (circa 1953) Granger,Washington	20	45	65

WRIGHT&McGILL

	poor-fair	good-vg	excellent
"Fre-line spin reel #16	3	5	10
Gold single action fly reel (c.1960)	4	7	14
"Stream & Lake" spinning reel	3	6	12

YAWMAN & ERBE

	poor-fair	good-vg	excellent
"Yawman & Erbe" auto. 1888,91 patent (key wind)	20	40	75
"Yawman & Erbe" auto. fly reel 1880 patent (no key)	25	50	85

J.W. YOUNG (England)

	poor-fair	good-vg	excellent
"Beaudex" fly reels (c.1960 and later)	12	28	45
"Beaudex" with rectangular line guide (c.1930-1950)	15	35	70
"Condex" fly reels	10	20	35
"Pridex" fly reels	10	20	35
"Landex" salmon fly reels (twin knobs)	15	40	85

ZEBCO

	poor-fair	good-vg	excellent
Cardinal spinning reels #4,5 (made in Sweden)	9	25	45
Ultralight size #3 Cardinal spinning reel (c.1970)	10	35	60
800 series spinning reels (c.1965)	2	4	8
Model 22 (early Zebco spin cast) c.1950	3	6	12
Model 33 all metal (early)	3	7	15
Model 310,330 baitcasting multipliers	3	5	10
Zero Hour Bomb reel	4	10	20

OTTO ZWARG

	poor-fair	good-vg	excellent
Big game reels in the Vom Hofe style (c.1940)	95	185	300
Silver, aluminum and hard rubber fly reel (#300)	175	350	700
Large multiplying salmon fly reel (#400)	350	750	1400